FACTS AND FALLACIES

CHRIS MORGAN and DAVID LANGFORD

FACTS AND FALLACIES

A Book of Definitive Mistakes and Misguided Predictions

St. Martin's Press
New York

Library of Congress Cataloging in Publication Data

Morgan, Chris.
    Facts and fallacies.

    1. History—Errors, inventions, etc.
2. Forecasting—History—Miscellanea.   I. Langford,
David.   II. Title.
D10.M66   909   81-14590
ISBN 0-312-27959-0   AACR2

Contents

To the 'Pieria' writers' group, who have a lot to answer for

Science should leave off making pronouncements; the river of knowledge has too often turned back on itself.

Sir James Jeans, *The Mysterious Universe*, 1930

The great tragedy of science—the staying of a beautiful hypothesis by an ugly fact.

T. H. Huxley

The human race, to which so many of my readers belong, has been playing at children's games from the beginning, and will probably do it till the end, which is a nuisance for the few people who grow up. And one of the games to which it is most attached is called, 'Keep tomorrow dark', and which is also named (by the rustics in Shropshire, I have no doubt) 'Cheat the Prophet'. The players listen very carefully and respectfully to all that the clever men have to say about what is to happen in the next generation. The players then wait until all the clever men are dead, and bury them nicely. They then go and do something else. That is all. For a race of simple tastes, however, it is great fun.

G. K. Chesterton, *The Napoleon of Notting Hill*, 1904

The historian of the future is faced with a similar kind of difficulty to that confronting the historian of the remoter past. It is not so much the dearth of reliable evidence which troubles him—though there are, as we shall see, some distressing gaps in our chronological knowledge—as that the few authorities upon which he can rely with a fair amount of confidence are apt to contradict each other on important points.

R. C. Churchill, *A Short History of the Future*, 1955

The most savage controversies are those about matters as to which there is no good evidence either way. Persecution is used in theology, not in arithmetic.

Bertrand Russell

Next to being right in this world, the best of all things is to be clearly and definitely wrong.

T. H. Huxley

Introduction

The Earth was created in 4004 BC on Sunday October the twenty-first at nine o'clock in the morning

This is a book of wild shots.

Studying the predictions, generalizations and categorical statements which people—often people who should know better—love to make about past, present and future is a little like watching an archery contest. Shots are scattered about the target, some missing it altogether; more enthusiasm is generated when someone hits the gold—H. G. Wells, for example, with his astonishing guess at the importance of tanks in future warfare ('The Land Ironclads', 1903). But let us be honest with ourselves: the greatest enjoyment in this sober competition comes when someone's arrow whizzes off at forty-five degrees from the intended line to transfix a nearby cow. This unholy glee is all the greater should the unfortunate archer be a reputed expert or the local mayor, or—better still—both.

In times when the universal fashion is to spurn the target and impale the cow, there is less fun in our man's colossal mistake. To babble about making gold when alchemy was in its heyday was hardly such a feat as to earn undying fame; it's much more interesting to learn that a Dr Girtanner of Göttingen said late in the eighteenth century that modern chemistry would do it yet:

> I n the *nineteenth century* the transmutation of metals will be generally known and practised. Every chemist and every artist will *make gold*; kitchen utensils will be of silver, and even gold, which will contribute more than anything else to *prolong life*, poisoned at present by the oxides of copper, lead and iron, which we daily swallow with our food.

Quoted in Isaac Disraeli's *Curiosities of Literature*, 1791–3

Those determined to find mystic predictions in every saying of the ancients will have no trouble in interpreting 'Every chemist . . . will make gold' as foretelling the profitability of modern drug companies.

The ultimate in malicious glee comes when such a dictum, sonorous, categorical and wrong, issues from an acknowledged Great Man who really should know better. Scientific history in particular is littered with the bones of great men who chose to say that such-and-such could never be done—it is such a recurring phenomenon, like the periodic rush of lemmings to their doom, that Arthur C. Clarke was moved to formulate his well-known Law: 'When a distinguished but elderly scientist states that something is possible, he is almost certainly right. When he states that something is impossible, he is very probably wrong.' (*Profiles of the Future*, 1962)

A famous example was provided by Simon Newcomb, one of the most celebrated American astronomers, who, in keeping with the scientific climate *circa* 1900, wrote the flat and final statement that manned aircraft were forever impossible. Meanwhile the Wright brothers, unlearned men who would not have recognized a scientific climate had it bitten them in the leg, were displaying their ignorance by suicidal yet successful flights above the sands at Kitty Hawk. Naturally Newcomb soon heard of this; now was the time for a graceful withdrawal from that particular field of prophecy. Newcomb, unfortunately, was maddened into proclaiming that, even if manned flight could be achieved by some unfair trick, nothing was more certain than that powered aircraft could never carry both a pilot and a passenger.

Moving from science to art, we find John Betjeman, ignoring Sturgeon's Law ('ninety per cent of everything is rubbish') and the evidence of human achievement in every field of art, producing the immortal statement that the wonders of colour and stereoscopy would make cinema our leading artform, and that bad films would be *impossible* (1935). In politics we have Leon Trotsky, less prophet than wishful thinker, explaining in 1925 that England was now ripe for revolution. (Contemporary novels echoed this, and we find Bertie Wooster philosophically accepting that one day his blood will be running down the gutters of Mayfair, with Jeeves blandly officiating at the guillotine.)

The quotations in this book have been selected to amuse and amaze, and even to provoke an occasional thought on human fallibility—not to mention the sweeping statements which today's eminent men are getting away with ... for now. Just as the compilers of that eccentric work *The Stuffed Owl: An Anthology of Bad Verse* were evilly careful to include the lapses of the greatest poets, so we have preferred to pick on the eminent, but some things are too wild and wonderful to omit. In *The Stuffed Owl* many lesser poets achieve a truly great badness, including one who deserves a place here for the interesting piece of hydrostatics which Macaulay termed 'the worst similitude in the world':

> The soul, aspiring, pants its source to mount,
> As streams meander level with their fount.

Robert Montgomery, 'The Omnipresence of the Deity'

We omit mere folklore, like the oft-heard 'scientists proved bumblebees can't fly'. Here the point was that classical aero-dynamics worked perfectly well for fixed-wing planes but could not cope with bees. No scientist ever stood before a press conference to deliver the grave announcement that, despite our foolish ancestors' beliefs, the bee cannot fly; any more than Isaac Newton, whose classical mechanics is inapplicable to nuclear doings, ever amazed the world by showing it was impossible for the sun to shine.

Why do people do it? What prompts them to babble predictions, comments and categorical statements which so often, and so often hilariously, come to grief? The reasons mostly boil down to a mixture of knowing too little and knowing too much (in older days they would have said ignorance and pride). The inevitable quotation is 'a little learning is a dangerous thing . . .'. Aristotle and countless later thinkers knew perfectly well that women were inferior beings, this learning being built into the Greek culture like a major roof-beam complete with dry rot. So it was unnecessary to conduct actual observations before making anatomical pro-nouncements, since woman the inferior would naturally have fewer teeth and darker blood than men and, what is more, Aristotle said so. This was good enough for everyone else for some centuries. Such cunning lack of logic was later applied to women so ridiculous as to ask for the vote. The first, the fundamental axiom was that it was wholly ridiculous for women to think or to vote, and the highly reasonable arguments started from this assumption in order to prove it anew. Women were pure spiritual beings, far too sweet to be corrupted by the vile business of politics; women were impractical beings unable to cope with complexities like remem-bering which party to vote for; women were over-emotional beings who at the drop of a crinoline might plunge the country into total war (something which men, of course, were good at avoiding).

Facts are trifling things compared with the immense weight of what one knows 'instinctively', soaked up through the pores from surrounding prejudices: that women are second-class citizens, coloured people not nice to know; that criminal behaviour is caused by Original Sin (so prisons do no good and we should simply shoot the swine); that the skies are constantly patrolled by alien intelligences in flying saucers. In a recent survey, London commuters were asked whether they felt that creatures from outer space watched them and knew their every thought: fully ten per cent said without hesitation, 'Yes.'

But surely scientists, trained to study facts objectively, could never succumb to the force of myth and preconception? Unfortunately a little learning remains dangerous: the specialist who knows too much in his own field, and too little elsewhere, is overwhelmingly tempted to explain everything in terms of the theories and data he or she knows best. Newcomb, already mentioned, was an astronomer well acquainted with Newton's Law of Universal Gravitation, the single golden rule which kept the solar system ticking off its ellipses like a gigantic timepiece—a rule which in earthly terms, without the vast masses and velocities of astrophysics, meant that objects heavier than air which went up would swiftly and undoubtedly come down again. QED. The new science of aerodynamics had an answer to that, but Newcomb chose to hold fast to his prejudices, reminding one of Charles Fort's little parable from *New Lands* (1923):

> S ome night in October, 1492, and savages upon an island-beach are gazing out at lights they had never seen before. The indications are that voyagers from some other world are nearby. But the wise men explain ... They explain in terms of the familiar. For instance, after all that is spiritual in a fish passes away, the rest of him begins to shine nights. So there are three big, old, dead things out in the water . . . .

A scientist straying outside his field can also overdo the open-mindedness. (Who was it who said, 'The trouble with having an open mind is that people come along and put things in it'?) Crookes and Lodge, the hard-headed physicists, and Conan Doyle, the hard-headed doctor, were taken in by spiritualist frauds; only a few years ago the mathematician John Taylor fell for the endemic spoon-bending of the mid-1970s; even Darwin, in a mood of open-minded investigation, tried the experiment of playing the trombone to his tulips (with negative results).

The special knowledge which clouds men's minds and distorts mere facts need not be scientific. Religion is an old favourite. There is a lunatic fundamentalism which insists that, since the Bible refers to 'the four corners of the world', our planet must be flat and square (adherents to this tenet seemingly fail to realize that a tetrahedron, a triangular-based pyramid, also satisfies the condition; but of course the earth has to be *flat*, otherwise the benighted Australians would not be able to see Christ's descent from the heavens on the Day of Judgement ...). There is a more subtle egoism which insists that earth, as God's special plaything, must occupy the exact centre of the universe with everything else going around it, no matter how complex and ludicrous this makes the orbits of the planets. Faint noises of 'I told you so' may still be emanating from the graves of these geocentrists following the adoption of modern cosmology, whereby any and every point of our universe can be considered as the centre. Religion has also wasted much time, from the scientific viewpoint, as theologians debated on the resurrection of cannibals (if a cannibal's body consists wholly of matter from others' bodies, what will be left to reconstitute him when they all reclaim their flesh on Judgement Day?) or the cosmically important problem of whether Adam had a navel. Sir Thomas Browne, that seventeenth-century rationalist, was unhappy with the notion of Adam's possessing 'that tortuosity or complicated nodosity we usually call the Navell', since this would mean that, unthinkably, 'the Creator affected superfluities or ordained parts without use or office'. It is not known what Sir Thomas thought of the appendix, body hair or the vestigial male nipples; possibly he found his own useful. As late as 1944 a US Congressional subcommittee went along with Sir Thomas, condemning the US Forces pamphlet *The Races of Mankind* on such grounds as that, oh horror, 'Adam and Eve are depicted with navels'.

Politics, too, can have unfortunate effects on rationality. Soviet biology suffered for years when the theories of Trofim D. Lysenko were adopted as the Party line on genetics—a form of genetics which dispensed with complicated concepts such as genes. The reason seems to have been that Lysenkoism agreed better with Marxist historical theory than the random gene-shuffling favoured in the West: Lysenko followed Lamarck in holding that acquired characteristics were inherited, or, to put it crudely, that by pulling wings off flies and subsequently mating them you would eventually breed wingless flies. In the same way, it is a notorious fact that the children of amputees tend to be short of limbs. This theory's only problem is a failure to agree with the facts; later it was quietly dropped. Similarly, Soviet geophysics is only now beginning to break loose from 1937 theories of internal dialectical conflict in the earth: 'Long periods of suppressed struggle ... are followed by a revolutionary phase' (M. A. Usov). Or, as the magazine *New Scientist* observed, 'As with the proletariat, the forces of containment in the earth were within the upper crust'.

A much sillier contention was Hans Hörbiger's World Ice Theory, which like many a crank belief was semi-officially adopted by the Nazi regime to the detriment of serious astronomy. All planets, it seems, are covered by miles-deep ice layers; great blocks of ice are constantly lurching about the solar system, falling earthwards as mere hailstorms but causing sunspots millions of miles across when they hit the sun; the earth is the solitary exception in this universe of ice-coated worlds, and the most complex parts of the theory are devoted to explaining why this should be so. The Reich also adopted hollow-earth theories (including one holding that we live on the *inner* surface, which led to a tense experiment whereby infrared cameras were trained at forty-five degrees into the air to photograph the British Fleet, anchored some way 'up' the concave slope of the earth's interior), and some infamous anthropology whose scientific conclusions regarding the wonderful Nordic and vile Semitic races are only too well known.

Or, again, our scientist hero may have his living to defend. For forty years his universe has been built on the immutability of Newton's laws of motion; the absoluteness of mathematical space and mathematical time are like the secure walls of his very own house. Then some wretched young fellow called Einstein turns up and casually remarks that space is bent; that time, like a lazy workman, runs at different rates depending on how you watch it. With a cry of joy and enthusiasm the elder scientist accepts the new axioms . . .

No. Human nature is such that he digs his heels in, not always for long (Einstein's rewrite of Newton was very swiftly praised and accepted); he knows nothing but that this outlandish theory cannot be right, and he comes out with such trenchant criticisms as 'This theory is nonsense', 'This theory is not to my taste', or 'Anyway, the man's a Jew'.

Many blundering statements do not even result from such pressures as the above. People are all too willing to be fools in the absence of the least religious, social or political bias, or of personal vested interest; sometimes they know nothing whatever but still feel the urge towards speculation . . . Hence such profound scientific thought as that of the Duchess of Newcastle (1624–74), who is said to have kept ladies-in-waiting constantly at hand to jot down her poetic inspirations at any hour of the day or night. Her meditation on the nature of liquid is surely immortal:

A ll that doth flow we cannot liquid name,
Or else would fire and water be the same;
But that is liquid which is moist and wet;
Fire that propriety can never get:
Then 'tis not cold that doth the fire put out,
But 'tis the wet that makes it die, no doubt.

from *What is Liquid?*

With similar awesome ignorance, President Hoover suggested to the USA Patents Office in 1922 that they might as well disband themselves: everything had been invented. (Other examples of this thinking appear in our Inventions chapter.) In such an intellectual vacuum it is easy for travellers' tales to rush in and breed like flies. Thus, keeping to the subject of flies, the 'spontaneous generation' of maggots in meat led in the early days of science to theories of what could spontaneously generate what. Example: To generate eels, you need something long and thin and eel-like, Hairs from horses' tails are long and thin, if not all that eel-like; what's more, eels are seen in the very same streams from which horses drink. Thus, to generate spontaneous eels, you need only put a few such hairs in water, and wait. If you get no eels you have *performed the experiment wrongly*; you lose one scientific status point and are condemned to try again until somehow you produce eels and thus establish scientific credibility. The great advantage of theories like this is that they cannot be disproved.

The ultimate such invincible theory came from Philip Gosse's book *Omphalos* (1857). This overcame all conflict between evolution and the Bible by explaining that God, despite actually creating the earth in six days, *circa* 4004BC, had cunningly covered his tracks by forging elaborate geological and palaeontological records which could tempt misguided scientists into believing all sorts of nonsense like natural selection or the accepted age of the earth. Perhaps this was a test of faith; but, despite the unassailability of his theory (each missing piece of evidence for biblical creation is further proof of God's ingenuity in covering things up), Gosse found that neither evolutionists nor fundamentalists had any faith in it.

We are back in the world of cranks. A theory invulnerable to any and all examples is a crank theory; scientific theories stick their necks out, make predictions, are modified or refuted if those predictions fail. One theory of the vaguer sort is called the Rule of Mediocrity, not an assessment of people or even of scientists, but a handy cosmological assumption to the effect that physical laws are much the same elsewhere and elsewhen; that our corner of the universe is a fairly typical suburb. As originally intended, this makes sense, but people can fall down disastrously by assuming a Rule of Mediocrity whereby tomorrow must be much like today and there is nothing new under the sun. This is what Clarke called the failure of nerve and of imagination; those who swear by it too loudly are condemned to a certain mediocrity of their own. Conversely, you can be over-optimistic about change, extrapolating with all the vigour of Freeman Dyson explaining in 1968 that we shall be able to fund starships with no trouble, eventually:

Our gross national product is far from being a fixed quantity. If the human race continues its economic growth rate of about 4% a year, we shall have a GNP a thousand times its present size in 200 years. When the GNP is multiplied by a thousand, the building of a ship for 100 billion dollars will seem like building a ship for 100 million dollars today . . . .

Ignoring such considerations as that inflation is running at a mite more than four per cent (so one hundred billion dollars might not be worth too much in two hundred years), or even that there could be a few more people to divide it between, it is obvious that in this compound-interest juggling Dyson is like a bacillus in a culture-dish calculating that, by fissioning every hour, its progeny will outweigh the earth in mere days. Unfortunately the food tends to run out first, leading to an obvious parallel with our own food and energy supplies.

But this book is a source of wry smiles rather than quivers of nameless dread. Here on the left are our learned and eminent persons, mingled with lesser-known ones and a scattering of outright lunatics. Here on the right are several hundred banana-skins, each carefully tested to the appropriate British Standard. Can our contestants survive to the end of the book without making fools of themselves?

Read on . . .

David Langford

The Arts

He bores me. He ought to have stuck to his flying machines.

Auguste Renoir, on Leonardo da Vinci

Literature we deal with separately, but other artforms have plenty of scope for oddity. Strange things can happen in paintings:

In his renowned oil painting *Israelites Gathering Manna In the Wilderness*, the painter Tintoretto armed Moses' men with shotguns. The earliest known gun did not appear until 1326, somewhat after the Exodus.

The Book of Lists

Still, this seems inherently more probable than that—as was seriously suggested a few years ago— the Israelites were fed during their wilderness wanderings by a nuclear-powered manna-manufacturing device donated by a friendly alien. Some people will believe anything.

Rembrandt is not to be compared in the painting of character with our extraordinarily gifted English artist, Mr Rippingille.

John Hunt (1775–1848)

I have seen and heard much of cockney impudence before now; but never expected to hear a coxcomb ask two hundred guineas for flinging a pot of paint in the public's face.

John Ruskin, of Whistler's 1878 exhibition

And the next century will be yet more critical than this. Every one of the fine arts will be more generally and more subtly appreciated than now.

T. Baron Russell, *A Hundred Years Hence*, 1905

And, to prove it, herewith is the definitive statement on the Nude in Art:

I don't discriminate between nude women, whether or not they are art. It's all lustful to me.

Chairman of Georgia State Literature Commission, USA

Luckily the ever-imaginative Nazis were able to offer a substitute:

The most perfect shape, the sublimest image that has recently been created in Germany has not come out of any artist's studio. It is the steel helmet.

SS officer Count Baudissin

Hitler himself had strong and clearly defined views, few of them connected with the arts. However, he did once unbend enough to offer an opinion on painting, and another on the theatre:

As for the degenerate artists, I forbid them to force their so-called experiences upon the public. If they do see fields blue, they are deranged, and should go to an asylum. If they only pretend to see them blue, they are criminals, and should go to prison.

1939

In no country is Shakespeare so badly acted as in England.

Table Talk, **1941**

From the theatre to the cinema, and thus to one of the most glorious predictions we have found:

Colour and stereoscopy will make the cinema into the greatest art in the world. Bad films will be impossible.

John Betjeman, 1935

The cinema, of course, has its own unusual problems: like the theatre, it suffers or used to suffer from censorship:

This film is apparently meaningless, but if it has any
meaning it is doubtless objectionable.

British Board of Film Censors, banning Jean Cocteau's
***The Seashell and the Clergyman*, 1956**

In the USA an elaborate Code of Practice for the cinema was drawn
up:

The use of liquor in American life, when not required
by the plot or for proper characterisation, will not be
shown.

***Motion Picture Production Code*, 1930**

The 1956 version of the code actually enshrined the famous saying
'Black tits aren't dirty, they're documentary':

Indecent or undue exposure is forbidden.
(a) The foregoing shall not be interpreted to exclude
actual scenes photographed in a foreign land of the
natives of that land, showing native life, provided:
(1) Such scenes are included in a documentary film or
travelogue depicting exclusively such land, its
customs and civilisation; and
(2) Such scenes are not in themselves intrinsically
objectionable.

***Motion Pictures Association Production Code*, 1956**

Then we have the broadcasting media:

Radio has no future.
Lord Kelvin, President of the Royal Society 1890-5

Radio, indeed, was surrounded with a haze of doubt in its origins.
Hertz, who first produced radio waves, doubted that they would be
any good for communication; and Marconi's plans to broadcast
across the Atlantic were said to be ridiculous because of the
curvature of the Earth (and so they were—but luckily the waves
bounced back off the ionosphere instead of vanishing into space,
and so crossed the Atlantic after all). As a tranquillizer, radio had
potential:

I can see the nerve doctor of the future saying to the
man with a nagging wife, 'Give her a radio set'.

Sir Eric Geddes, 1926

But some were convinced that the novelty would soon wear off:

> I am reported to be 'pessimistic' about broadcasting, though the truth is that I have anticipated its complete disappearance—confident that the unfortunate people, who must now subdue themselves to 'listening-in', will soon find a better pastime for their leisure.
>
> **H. G. Wells, *The Way the World is Going*, 1928**

Television, being even newer, was denounced more vigorously:

> Television won't matter in your lifetime or mine.
>
> **Rex Lambert, *The Listener*, editorial, 1936**

> Television won't last. It's a flash in the pan.
>
> **Mary Somerville, pioneer of radio educational broadcasts, 1948**

And even now it is hard to refute this last and most damning observation:

> Television? No good will come of this device. The word is half Greek and half Latin.
>
> **C. P. Scott (1846–1932)**

Astronomy

People give ear to an upstart astrologer [Copernicus] who strove to show that the earth revolves, not the heavens or the firmament, the sun and the moon. Whoever wishes to appear clever must devise some new system, which of all systems is of course the very best. This fool wishes to reverse the entire science of astronomy; but sacred Scripture tells us that Joshua commanded the sun to stand still, and not the earth.

Martin Luther

Bertrand Russell quotes this and goes on:

Melancthon was equally emphatic; so was Calvin, who after quoting the text: 'The world also is established, that it cannot be moved' (Psalms *xciii*, 1) triumphantly concluded: 'Who will venture to place the authority of Copernicus above that of the Holy Spirit?' Even Wesley, so late as the 18th century, while not daring to be quite so emphatic, nevertheless stated that the new doctrines in astronomy 'tend toward infidelity'.

Basking in the cheery glow of modern scientific complacency, we may now consider that Copernicus was right and the conservatives wrong; that the earth does indeed go round the sun, and that this is the ultimate, absolute truth. As it happens, the controversy was even more of a storm in a teacup than it seems; because *it doesn't matter*. It is perfectly possible to describe the motions of all the planets relative to a 'stationary' earth; the equations are a good deal simpler if you assume, as a mathematical fiction, that the planets all go round a stationary sun; but certain people would have none of it even as a fiction.

The first proposition, that the sun is the centre and does not revolve about the earth, is foolish, absurd, false in theology, and heretical, because expressly contrary to Holy Scripture. ... The second proposition, that the earth is not the centre, but revolves about the sun, is absurd, false in philosophy, and, from a theological point of view at least, opposed to true faith.

The Inquisition, on Galileo's proposals

The opinion of the earth's motion is of all heresies the most abominable, the most pernicious, the most scandalous; the immovability of the earth is thrice sacred; argument against the immortality of the soul, the existence of God, and the Incarnation, should be tolerated sooner than an argument to prove that the earth moves.

Father Melchior Inchofer, a Jesuit, 1632

We will add only that Father Inchofer seemed to have some odd priorities. Nor was it only the hard-liners of the Roman Catholic Church who adhered to the idea of a geocentric universe: towards the middle of the next century works of reference in Protestant England still remained adamant on the subject of a fixed earth.

PLANETS are wandering stars, that have their proper motion from east to west, and do not always keep the same distances between one another, as the fixed stars do in the firmament, each of which have their orb or circle wherein they make their revolution; their number is seven, *viz.* Saturn, Jupiter, Mars, the Sun, Venus, Mercury, and the Moon. . . . Astronomers compute that the Sun is 166 times as big as the earth, Saturn 91, Jupiter 95, Mars much about the size of the earth, Venus 1/38 part of it, Mercury 1/2000 part, and the Moon 1/40.

Thomas Dyche & William Pardon, *A New General English Dictionary,* **1744**

More recent thinkers have shown that the stars are motionless:

Nothing can be more certain than that the stars have not changed their declinations or latitudes *one degree* in the last 71¾ years.

Captain Woodley, RN, 1834

While, in this very century, the hasty conclusions of Copernicus, Galileo and the rest have been challenged with a new argument of irrefutable strength, showing that the earth does not rotate:

If the Earth did move at tremendous speed, how could we keep a grip on it with our feet? We could walk only very, very slowly; and should find it slipping rapidly under our footsteps. Then, which way is it turning? If we walked in the direction of its tremendous speed, it would push us on terribly rapidly. But if we tried to walk against its revolving—? Either way we should be terribly giddy, and our digestive processes impossible.

Margaret L. S. Missen, *The Sun Goes Round the Earth*, 1950s

Our second lady iconoclast does not *believe* in the fuel-free transport system she suggests below—this, you must understand, is biting sarcasm:

An aircraft flying at this rate [1,000kph] in the same direction as that of the rotation could not cover any ground at all. It would remain suspended in mid-air above the spot from which it took off, since both speeds are equal. There would, in addition, be no need to fly from one place to another situated on the same latitude. The aircraft could just rise and wait for the desired country to arrive in the ordinary course of the rotation, and then land; although it is difficult to see how any plane could manage to touch ground at all on an airfield which is slipping away at the rate of 1,000kph. It might certainly be useful to know what people who fly think of the rotation of the Earth.

Mme Gabrielle Henriet, *Heaven & Earth*, 1957

Besides being so constantly accused of twirling around a motionless earth, the sun has other problems—such as not being hot.

The most recent observations confirm the supposition that the Sun is a black, opaque body, with a luminous and incandescent atmosphere, through which the solar body is often seen in black spots, frequently of enormous dimensions.

John Timbs, *Things Not Generally Known*, 1857

(Concerning sunspots, Galileo had annoyed Catholic teachers by seeing them through his telescope, thus implying that God's work had blemishes: Catholic universities were forbidden to mention sunspots, some keeping them dark for centuries . . .) But, since the sun is such a cool and shady place, it could well be inhabited.

I f (says Arago) this question were simply proposed to me, Is the Sun inhabited? I should reply, that I know nothing about the matter. But let any one ask of me if the Sun can be inhabited by beings organised in a manner analogous to those which people our globe, and I hesitate not to reply in the affirmative. The existence in the Sun of a central obscure nucleus, enveloped in an opaque atmosphere far beyond which the luminous atmosphere exists, is by no means opposed, in effect, to such a conception.

Sir William Herschel thought the Sun to be inhabited . . .

John Timbs, *ibid*.

Both Arago and Herschel were noted astronomers: Herschel went on to give dubious 'proofs' that the sun was cold, based on such facts as the increased coldness of our air at higher altitudes (i.e., nearer the sun). Yes, the sun could be 'abundantly stored with inhabitants'. After all

W hatever the sun may be, it is certainly not a ball of flaming gas.

D. H. Lawrence

T he popular notion that the Sun is on fire is rubbish, and merely a hoary superstition, on a par with a belief in a flat earth, an earth resting on the back of a tortoise or an elephant, or a sun revolving around a stationary earth . . . It rests on no sure basis of evidence; and if it is discarded, great simplification becomes possible in the sciences of astronomy, geology and physics, and many other branches of science can be placed on surer foundations.

Reverend P. H. Francis, *The Temperate Sun*, 1970

I f the sun is a hot body, it is improbable that life on earth will exist tomorrow.

***Ibid*.**

The Reverend Francis showed also that stars were merely reflections of the sun in the interestingly curved and shiny surface of 'infinity':

No star has a real existence, any more than the image of a candle in a mirror has a real existence.

The Mathematics of Infinity, 1968

Others, while conceding that stars might well exist, felt that they were forever unknowable, or quite close at hand, or incapable (like the sun) of staying alight:

We see how we may determine their forms, their distances, their bulk, their motions, but we can never know anything of their chemical or mineralogical structures . . .

Auguste Comte, *Cours de Philosophie Positive*, 1835

(Within fifty years of Comte's death the spectroscope had been invented, so the 'chemical structure' of the stars could be ascertained.)

When astronomers tell me that a star is so far off that its light takes a thousand years to reach us, the magnitude of the lie seems to me inartistic.

George Bernard Shaw, quoted by G. K. Chesterton, 1910

No possible combination of terrestrial elements can give the combination of high radiation and staying power which is observed in the sun and stars.

J. H. Jeans, *Eos*, 1931

Comets too were the subject of much controversy—quite apart from their tendency to predict catastrophes:

The heathen write that the comet may arise from natural causes, but God creates not one that does not foretoken a sure calamity.

Martin Luther

One eminent cleric seemed to think that, on the whole, comets were probably meteors:

C omets are not heavenly bodies, but originate in the earth's atmosphere below the moon; for everything heavenly is eternal and incorruptible, but comets have a beginning and ending—*ergo*, comets cannot be heavenly bodies.

Father Augustion de Angelis of the Clementine College, Rome, 1673

Meteors, on the other hand, were most certainly not meteors:

O n 13 Sept, 1768, people in fields near Luce, France, saw a stone-mass drop from the sky after a violent thunderclap. The great physicist, Lavoisier, who knew better than any peasant that this was impossible, reported to the Academy of Science that the witnesses were mistaken or lying. Despite historical and contemporary evidence, the Academy would not accept the reality of meteorites until 1803 . . .

Fortean Times

In America, country of reason, it was all a matter of balancing the evidence:

I could more easily believe that two Yankee professors would lie than that stones would fall from heaven.

Thomas Jefferson, 1807

Possibly so; but if one wants to discover the real truth about meteors one should consult a dictionary:

M ETEORS are imperfect mixtures of the elements, drawn up by the sun and so variously formed into comets or blazing stars, or other strange appearances in the air, as *ignes fatui*, &c. but more ordinarily into hail, snow, and hoary frost.

Thomas Dyche & William Pardon, *A New General English Dictionary*, 1744

Our favourite theory of astronomy and cosmology is Hörbiger's famous World Ice Theory, summarized in our introduction. Hitler too was a fan:

I'm quite well inclined to accept the cosmic theories of Hörbiger. It's not impossible, in fact, that ten thousand years before our era there was a clash between the earth and the moon that gave the moon its present orbit. It's likewise possible that the earth attracted to it the atmosphere which was that of the moon, and that this radically transformed the condition of life on our planet. One can imagine that, before this accident, man could live at any altitude—for the simple reason that he was not subject to the constraint of atmospheric pressure.

Adolf Hitler, *Table Talk*, 1942

Other such cosmic collisions have also been proposed: Immanuel Velikovsky, for example, suggested an insanely complex series of collisions, near-misses and interactions between comets and planets, many involving electrical forces hitherto unknown, which between them account for every major Biblical event from the fall of Jericho (earthquake) to the plague of Egypt (nasty things dropping from a comet) and the manna in the wilderness (nice things dropping from the same comet). Life is too short to discuss all the sillinesses of these doctrines.

More inherently plausible was the theory of George Darwin (fifth son of Charles), who estimated that the moon had once been part of the earth and even that the Pacific Ocean might well be the hole left when the moon parted company with us. This, though jolly, has been quite thoroughly discredited. For ourselves, we prefer the enchanting simplicity and aloofness from logic of the World Ice cosmology ... but Hörbiger's followers have been strangely silent of late. Perhaps this is why:

The final proof of the whole cosmic ice theory will be obtained when the first landing on the ice-coated surface of the Moon takes place.

Hörbiger Institute pamphlet, 1953

Aviation

Providence has given to the French the empire of the land, to the English that of the sea, and to the Germans that of the air.

Jean-Paul Richter (1763–1825)

Aviation began with the Montgolfier balloon of 1783. The first manned balloon went up in the same year, but some people were unimpressed even after several more flights:

We know a method of mounting into the air, and, I think, are not likely to know more ... I had rather now find a medicine that can ease an asthma.

Dr Samuel Johnson, 1784

Charles Darwin's grandfather, Erasmus, on the other hand, was filled with optimism and became lyrical about prospects still a century in the future:

Soon shall thy arm, unconquered steam, afar
Drag the slow barge, or drive the rapid car;
Or on wide-waving wings expanded bear
The flying chariot through the field of air.

Erasmus Darwin, *The Botanic Garden*, 1791

Admittedly, the steam-'plane never did materialize; but hordes of eminent men would have done better to imitate Darwin's enthusiasm. Instead, the comments on flying machines other than balloons became more and more pessimistic.

Heavier-than-air flying machines are impossible.

Lord Kelvin, President of the Royal Society, 1890–5

The demonstration that no possible combination of known substances, known forms of machinery and known forms of force, can be united in a practical machine by which men shall fly 'long distances through the air, seems to the writer as complete as it is possible for the demonstration to be.

Simon Newcomb, *c.* 1900

Flight by machines heavier than air is unpractical and insignificant, if not utterly impossible.

Ibid., 1902

As mentioned in our introduction, Newcomb was a celebrated astronomer, learned in the ways of empty space and gigantic masses, and thus peculiarly qualified to pontificate on doing things within the atmosphere. The fatal year of 1903 came round; at Kitty Hawk the Wright brothers were industriously tinkering with their prototypes; and Newcomb announced:

Aerial flight is one of that class of problems with which man will never be able to cope.

He was not alone.

We hope that Professor Langley will not put his substantial greatness as a scientist in further peril by continuing to waste his time, and the money involved, in further airship experiments. Life is too short, and he is capable of services to humanity incomparably greater than can be expected to result from trying to fly ... For students and investigators of the Langley type there are more useful employments.

New York Times, 10 December, 1903

Just seven days later the Wrights' first powered machine flew, but the mood of scepticism was so great that newspapers refused to accept that they had actually done so. Newspapers, indeed, were generally unwilling to print 'this ridiculous story' until weeks after. When the truth was eventually established, Newcomb at once thrust his foot further into his mouth by declaring that, at any rate, it would be impossible for both a pilot and a passenger to be carried. The Wrights duly went on to achieve a two-man flight, in 1904, whereupon the engineer (and, later, aviation pioneer) Octave Chanute commented:

This machine may even carry mail in special cases. But the useful loads will be very small. The machines will eventually be fast, they will be used in sport, but they are not to be thought of as commercial carriers.

Only ten years later the first regular internal passenger service was established in the USA. Chanute was rewarded by having an airfield named after him, though he was by no means alone in his opinions:

A s it is not at all likely that any means of suspending the effect of air-resistance can ever be devised, a flying-machine must always be slow and cumbersome ... But as a means of amusement, the idea of aerial travel has great promise. Small one-man flying machines or the aerial counterpart of tandem bicycles, will no doubt be common enough. We shall fly for pleasure.

T. Baron Russell, *A Hundred Years Hence,* **1905**

Apparently the facts of aerial life also took an absurdly long time to cross the Atlantic and, incredible though it seems, it is reported that the Edwardian war minister, Lord Haldane, said, 'The aeroplane will never fly'—in 1907! A few years after that, another celebrated astronomer pooh-poohed the possibility of passenger services:

T he popular mind often pictures gigantic flying machines speeding across the Atlantic carrying innumerable passengers in a way analogous to our modern steam-ships ... it seems safe to say that such ideas are wholly visionary, and even if a machine could get across with one or two passengers, the expense would be prohibitive to any but the capitalist who could use his own yacht.

William H. Pickering, 1910

In 1909 Louis Bleriot flew his monoplane to England, causing some agitation to the Collector of Customs at Dover:

H on Sirs, I have to report that M. Bleriot, with his monoplane, successfully crossed the Channel from Calais this morning ...

A wireless message was conveyed to our offices announcing his departure, but he was flying at such a height that they could not trace him with a telescope.

I visited the spot where he landed at 6.30am, and got into conversation with an individual largely interested in the Wright aeroplane who gave it as his opinion that although airships will never come into commercial use, there are great possibilities in store for them, and I think that a time may come when this Department will have to treat their arrival seriously . . .

Report of the Collector, 25 July 1909

Fortunately the monoplane had been properly dealt with on arrival, and a resourceful officer had

interviewed M. Bleriot, & issued to him a Quarantine Certificate, thereby treating it as a yacht, & the aviator as Master & owner.

The Collector again takes up the tale:

I gave instructions to the Surveyor that the crossing of the Channel by airship was not to be treated officially by our officers, as I considered that an attempt to impose Customs regulations on anyone engaged in experiments with aerial navigation would only tend to bring this Department into ridicule without doing any practical good.

Those were the days.

Strange pronouncements since that time seem rarer:

The first real air-liner, carrying some five or six hundred passengers, will probably appear after or towards the end of the battle between fixed and moving-wing machines. And it will be a flying-boat.

Oliver Stewart, *Aeolus or the Future of the Flying Machine*, *c*. 1927

And when Frank Whittle was developing his jet engine before the war, he is reputed to have shown his design to the Professor of Aeronautical Engineering at Cambridge University, who after a single glance dismissed him with the comment,

Very interesting, Whittle, my boy, but it will never work!

In recent years the ecological aspects of aircraft have received more consideration:

> I remember an American said there is more upset to the ozone layer by cows breaking wind than by a whole fleet of supersonic transports flying simultaneously.

Archibald Russell, designer of Concorde, 1976

It may be true, it may be true.

Biology

I t is a ravening beast, feining itself gentle and tame, but being touched it biteth deep and poysoneth deadly.

Edward Topsell, *Historie of Foure Footed Beastes*, 1607

Thus described is the shrew, actually one of Britain's smallest and least offensive animals, but long believed poisonous. This illustrates the area of knowledge which has, over the ages, been subject to the most persistent errors and misconceptions – the natures and habits of animals.

Astonishingly, most animals involved were neither rare nor exotic but so common that these fallacies could easily have been corrected by observation, but the opinions of earlier writers were always accepted as the truth and repeated without question, from the ancient Greeks (Aristotle originated many errors) until the eighteenth century.

Thus it was long believed that badgers had the two legs on one side of their body shorter than the two on the other. The newt, somewhat smaller and less offensive than the shrew, was described as 'venomous'. Venison was thought poisonous in the summer, because deer were believed to feed on adders and other poisonous snakes, contaminating their flesh: it sounds like a story put about by landowners to discourage poachers. Very many early writers repeated the tale of goat's blood and its expensive tastes. As Sir Thomas Browne wrote in the seventeenth century:

W e hear it in every mouth, and many good Authors reade it, that a Diamonde, which is the hardest of stones, not yeelding unto Steele, Emery or any other thing, is yet made soft by the bloud of a Goat.

Perhaps all these early writers were too impoverished to test the statement.

St Patrick was credited with having destroyed all Irish spiders along with the snakes. This was firmly believed up until 1834, when evidence to the contrary was first published by Dr R. T. Templeton. In fact there are about three hundred species of spiders in Ireland. Could they possibly have been dismissed as hallucinations before the 1830s?

That toads were venomous and carried precious jewels inside their heads should quickly have been disproved by generations of those who must have killed toads in hope of gain but remained poor and unpoisoned, yet this story had its place in folklore for centuries. In the same way, the stories that bear-cubs were born as shapeless masses which had to be licked into shape by their mother, and that crocodiles always shed tears over their victims, were such familiar truths to our ancestors that allusions to them became part of the English language.

The pelican was believed to feed her young with her own blood, taken from her breast, and became a popular emblem of loving sacrifice. The truth is that pelicans frequently preen their breast feathers with their bills, which have a crimson spot on the tip. One of Aristotle's theories was that birds never urinate 'because that superfluity which could be converted into urine, is turned into feathers'.

It stands to reason that the way to avoid doubt, misconception or silliness regarding animals is to look them up in a work of reference. So we turned to our trusty dictionary—Thomas Dyche & William Pardon's *A New General English Dictionary* (1744)—and found the following:

R EPTILE any creature that crawls upon its belly, or that rests on one part thereof while it moves the other along, as a snake, earth-worm &c.

W ORM a creeping insect . . .

I NSECT any creature that flies or creeps, that is not divided into joints and limbs, but surrounded with rings or divisions, capable of being separated without destroying life, as worms, &c. or may have the head easily separated from the body, and yet remain alive for a long time after, as bees, flies, &c. there are a very great variety of these creatures, too tedious for me to enumerate.

What could be clearer than that? We are particularly fond of that definition of reptiles, which must include not only earthworms but also slugs, snails, seals, walruses, most shellfish, as well as those curious fish that like to emerge from the water and bask on mudbanks. From the same source:

M OTH a small flying insect that eats woollen-cloth in particular.

And just to show that Messrs Dyche & Pardon's grasp of human biology was at least as good as their entomology:

T ESTICLES the seminal organs in a man or woman.

With so many strange beliefs about concerning common animals, you will not be surprised to learn that non-European species were treated with even less regard for the truth. The lion (which, we are told, has black blood) was long regarded as the most generous and chivalrous of animals, and one which would never attack a woman.

T he hyaena was held to possess the power of counterfeiting man's speech, and of turning the gift to profitable account by going up at night to a shepherd's or woodman's hut and calling out the man's name. Upon the man's going forth to see who wanted him, he was promptly torn to pieces.

F. E. Hulme, *Natural History Lore and Legend*, 1895

The elephant was described by Saint Isidore, the seventh-century encyclopaedist, as being very similar in appearance to a goat, while Sebastian Munster, in the sixteenth century, shows a man using an elephant to pull a plough. Here the appearance of the animal is correct, though its size is about that of a Shetland pony.

A nother strange idea of the ancients was that the elephant when pursued by the hunters beats its tusks against the trees until they drop off, as he has a shrewd suspicion that it is his ivory rather than himself that they want.

Hulme, *ibid*.

The female elephant was long supposed to rear her young in deep water in order to avoid its being eaten by dragons. (One must not forget that only three or four centuries ago dragons were widely believed to be as real as elephants, or perhaps, by untravelled Europeans, slightly more so.)

O ur forefathers had a very real belief in the veritable existence of the dragon, not by any means regarding it as a symbol merely, a figure of speech or apt allegory, but as one of the quite definite perils that the adventurous traveller in distant lands might be called upon to face, while preparations of the dragon were a recognised feature in the pharmacopoeia.

The 'Annals of Winchester', for the year 1177, inform us that 'in this yeare Dragons were sene of many in England'. In 1274 it is recorded that there was an earthquake on the Eve of St Nicholas' Day, and that there appeared 'a fiery dragon which frightened the English'.

Hulme, *ibid.*

The great Arab traveller Leo Africanus, in *Descrittione dell'Africa* (1526), declares that the dragon is the progeny of the eagle and the wolf. Ulisses Aldrovandi, in his *History of Serpents and Dragons*, published in 1640, devotes fifty pages to the dragon, showing his belief in it by dealing with it there rather than in his *Historia Monstrorum*. Various unlikely forms of miscegenation are mentioned by Giambattista Della Porta (1541–1615):

P orta includes some strange animals in his treatise: thus the leopard is the offspring, according to him, of the panther and lioness; the crocuta of the hyaena and lioness; the thoes of the panther and the wolf; the jumar of the bull and ass; the musinus of the goat and ram; the cinirus of the he-goat and ewe.

Hulme, *ibid.*

Sir Thomas Browne, who was certainly not the most credulous of seventeenth-century writers, is confident in his acceptance of some beasts we now suspect to be mythical.

B ut although we deny not the existence of the Basilisk, yet whether we do not commonly mistake in the conception hereof, and call that a Basilisk which is none at all, is surely to be questioned. For certainly that which from the conceit of its generation we vulgarly call a Cockatrice, and wherein (but under a different name) we intend a formal Identity and adequate conception with the Basilisk; is not the Basilisk of the Ancients, whereof such wonders are delivered. For this of ours is generally described with legs, wings, a Serpentine and winding tail, and a crist or comb somewhat like a Cock. But the Basilisk of elder times was a proper kind of Serpent, not above three palms long, as some account; and differenced from other Serpents by advancing his head, and some white marks or coronary spots upon the crown, as all authentick Writers have delivered ... It is not impossible, what is affirmed of this animal, the visible rays of their eyes carrying forth the subtilest portion of their poison, which received by the eye of man or beast, infecteth first the brain, and is from thence communicated unto the heart.

Sir Thomas Browne, *Pseudodoxia Epidemica,* **1646**

Early bestiaries are full of animals which we, supercilious on account of our twentieth-century sophistication, tend to regard as the grossest of fantasies—the products of (presumably) some devious monastic mind. For example, the Bonacon was an animal like a bull, but with horns curled round so as to be useless. 'But,' in the words of the twelfth-century Cambridge Bestiary, 'however much his front end does not defend this monster, his belly end is fully sufficient. For when he turns to run away he emits a fart with the contents of his large intestine which covers three acres. And any tree that it reaches catches fire. Thus he drives away his pursuers with noxious excrement.'

Equally bizarre is this:

B urton and other early English writers thoroughly believe in the existence of tailed men, and it has long been an article of belief that divers men even in this realm of England were born with tails. The Devonshire men stoutly contended that their Cornish neighbours were thus distinguished.

Hulme, *ibid.*

Turning from the land to the sea, but staying with tailed people, we come to mermaids. Hulme quotes a Dutch account of a mermaid which drifted inland through a broken dyke and was taught to behave in a civilized manner. 'She learned to spinne and perform other pettie offices of women. She never spake, but lived dumbe, and continued alive fifteene yeares.'

When we read in another old author that 'in the island Mauritius they eat of the mermaid, its taste is not unlike veal', the last vestige of the poetry of the belief vanishes.

Hulme, *ibid.*

And hence to other marine exotica:

Hans Egede, the apostle of Greenland, encountered a sea-monster, of which he gives an account in his 'Journal of the Missions to Greenland'.
    'It raised itself,' he says, 'so high up out of the water that its head reached above our main-top.' He describes it as having a long, sharp snout and broad flippers, and as spouting water like a whale. Its body seemed covered with scales, its skin uneven and wrinkled, and its lower part formed like a snake. The creature after some time plunged back into the water, and then turned its tail up above the surface a whole ship's length from the head.

John Gibson, *Monsters of the Sea,* **1890**

Floating islands are invariably Krakens.

Bishop Erik Pontoppidan, *Natural History of Norway,*
1752–4

But can you be more specific than that?

Its back or upper part, says Pontoppidan, appears to be about a mile and a half in circumference, and at first resembles a number of small islands surrounded with something that floats about like seaweed. Here and there a larger rising, like a sand-bank, is observed, on which fishes of various sorts are seen continually leaping about till they roll off at the sides into the water. At least several bright points or horns appear, which grow in thickness the higher they rise above the surface of the water, and sometimes they stand up as high and as large as the masts of a middle-sized ship. These, it seems, are the creature's arms; and such is their strength, that if they seized the largest man-of-war they would infallibly drag it to the bottom.

After a short time at the surface, the kraken descends
as slowly as it rose; but even then the danger is not less
for any vessel within reach, as in sinking it displaces so
great a volume of water as to give rise to a whirlpool
capable, like that of the Maelstrom, of drawing
everything down with it.

Gibson, *ibid.*

Despite all this unstinting credulity, there was one kind of animal in
which the ancient and mediaeval writers did *not* believe, and which
they used in order to signify total impossibility, even alongside such
creatures as dragons and mermaids. This was a black swan. Of
course, when black swans were discovered in Australia, nobody
believed in them. Similarly, when the duck-billed platypus was
found in Australia and first brought back to Europe in the late
eighteenth century, it was declared to be a fake, rather crudely
stitched together from parts of other animals.

It is interesting to note that in 1812 Georges Cuvier (the 'Father
of Palaeontology') said, 'There is little hope of discovering new
species of large quadrupeds.' Since then several dozen have been
found, including antelopes, bears, the okapi, a species of ostrich, a
species of zebra, an eleven-foot monitor lizard . . .

We would not like you to think that all errors and misconceptions
about animals died out somewhere in the eighteenth century, when
people suddenly became modern and clever.

So lately as the year 1866 it came out at the inquest
held on the body of a child that had died of
hydrophobia, that one of the relatives fished up out of
the river the dead body of the dog that had done the
mischief, in order that its liver might be cooked and
eaten by the child In spite of this the patient died.

Hulme, *ibid.*

He can live anywhere, in any landscape, at any
altitude . . . He escapes the effects of cold and lack of
winter food by hibernating in caves or in pits . . . Such
creatures can run like horses, and swim rivers and fast
mountain torrents. In the process of transition to the
biped manner of movement, the females, unlike the
apes, developed long mammary glands, so, throwing

their breasts over their shoulders, they can, while
walking along, feed the young hanging from their backs.

Odette Tchernine, *The Yeti*, 1970

The examples that have been held up to us (in praise of
work) are a little unfortunate. 'How does the little
busy bee improve each shining hour, and gather honey
all the day from every opening flower?' Well, he does
not. He spends most of the day in buzzing and aimless
aerobatics, and gets about the fifth of the honey he would
collect if he organized himself.

Sir Heneage Ogilvie

Staying with bees, one of the most fascinating and long-lived of
animal beliefs has been in the spontaneous generation of insects and
similar small creatures from decaying or inanimate material.

So when the Oxe corrupteth into Bees, or the Horse
into Hornets, they come not forth in the image of
their originals. So the corrupt and excrementous
humours in man are animated into Lice.

Sir Thomas Browne, *ibid*.

But John Swan, in his *Speculum Mundi* (1635), maintains that this is
all wrong: it is a dead calf, of course, which produces bees, and a
mule which gives rise to hornets, while a dead horse can only bring
forth wasps (we wonder what it is that must kill so many horses
during the month of August), and humble bees will eventually
proceed from the decaying body of an ass. Now, are you quite clear
on that?

Many authors have averred that rats and mice would spring
spontaneously from any mass of putrefaction if it were left for long
enough. Diodorus Siculus (first century BC) was quite sure that
toads were generated by the heat of the sun from the dead bodies of
ducks putrefying in mud. Aelian (third century AD) declared that
once a dead man's marrow putrefied it turned into serpents, while
St Gregory of Tours (sixth century AD) had no doubts that, if some
of the herb basil was chewed and then laid in the sun, it would
produce serpents (and who would dare to contradict a saint?).
Giambattista Della Porta says, 'We have experienced also that the
hairs of a horse's mane laid in the waters become serpents, and our
friends have tried the same.' No less categorically he continues: 'No

man denies but that serpents are easily engendered of man's flesh, specially of his marrow.' Porta is also one of the authors who describes the curious origin of barnacle-geese:

S ome say [barnacles] come of worms, some of the boughs of trees which fall into the sea; if any of them be cast on shore, they die; but they which are swallowed still into the sea, live and get out of their shells, and grow to be ducks or such-like birds.

Natural Magic, **early seventeenth century**

B ARNACLE ... The French, on the coast of Normandy, have also barnacles, which they call *macreuse*, which produces a bird of the duck kind, which the French eat as fish, on fish days, tho' Mr. Ray has observed it to be a real fowl.

Dyche & Pardon, *ibid*.

How on earth, one must ask, were such wondrous things established? The answer must be the same as Dr Johnson's when asked by a lady why, in his *Dictionary of the English Language*, he defined the word 'pastern' as 'the knee of a horse' (whereas it is that part between fetlock and hoof). His reply was, 'Ignorance, madam, pure ignorance.'

Business

The avoidance of taxes is the only intellectual pursuit that still carries any reward.

John Maynard Keynes

Unfortunately economists tend to a certain vagueness of expression when speaking at large, while businessmen are either suspicious and reticent or so gross and excessive in their self-advertisement that they become tedious: we have no desire to fill this chapter with accounts of how each brand of soap-flakes washes whiter than all the others. Which is why this is a short chapter. But advertising offers a few small gems:

The trade of Advertising is now so near to perfection that it is not easy to propose any improvement.

The Idler, **1759**

It is quite possible, of course, that advertisements have indeed been going steadily downhill since 1759. From what Thomas Jefferson says, they must have been much more perfect in those days than now:

Advertisements contain the only truths to be relied on in a newspaper.

Thomas Jefferson (1743–1826)

In 1905 an unexpectedly responsible future was seen for them:

The intrinsic nature of the vastly-extended advertising of the new age will be influenced by the new growth of public intelligence. Once almost wholly, and now to a very great extent, addressed to the least intelligent faculties of the public—the faculties most liable to be influenced by large type and *ad captandum* phrasing—advertising will in the future world become gradually more and more intelligent in tone. It will seek to influence demand by argument instead of clamour, a tendency already more apparent every year. Cheap attention-calling tricks and clap-trap will be wholly replaced, as they are already being greatly replaced, by serious exposition; and advertisements, instead of being mere repetitions of stale catch-words, will be made interesting and informative, so that they will be welcomed instead of being shunned.

T. Baron Russell, *A Hundred Years Hence,* **1905**

But by 1922 they were virtually on their last legs.

Peasants and priests and all sorts of practical and sensible people are coming back into power . . . They will not be affected by advertisements, no more than the priests and peasants of the Middle Ages would have been affected by advertisements. Only a very soft-headed, sentimental and rather servile generation could possibly be affected by advertisements at all.

G. K. Chesterton, *What I Saw in America,* **1922**

Yes: although advertisement survives in a degraded form, it must be nearly done with. Even the petrol companies were becoming tired, a decade ago, of their free-gift campaigns:

If all other petrol companies ceased giving free gifts we would be the first to stop. As it is we must reluctantly continue.

Esso spokesman, *c.* **1970**

Much advertising material, not to mention less important business items, such as bills, orders, catalogues and specifications, need to be collected and distributed by some sort of centralized authority, with an efficiency which will increase to meet the more critical demands of the future:

And however rapidly and however frequently the trains or airships of the period may travel, the process of making up van loads of mail matter for despatch to remote centres, and redistribution there, is far too clumsy for what commerce will demand a hundred years hence. No doubt the soil of every civilised country will be permeated by vast networks of pneumatic tubes: and all letters and parcels will be thus distributed at a speed hardly credible today.

T. Baron Russell, *ibid.*

43

Yes, perhaps the people of 1905 would scarcely believe the great speed with which today's mail is lost, left standing in railway waggons, or misdelivered.

Business efficiency in general is of course determined not only by productivity but by the amount of time one spends on strike or paralysed through somebody else's trade dispute.

> What will happen a hundred years hence is that trade disputes will have disappeared because all the workers will be practically their own employers . . . the workers in every industry being paid, not by fixed wages, but by a share in the produce of their labour.
>
> **T. Baron Russell,** *ibid*.

Passing quickly over the widespread strikes which are raging in Poland even as we write, let us see what the top managers have to say for themselves:

> This company is not bust. We are merely in a cyclical decline.
>
> **Lord Stokes, Chairman of British Leyland, 1974**

> I think there is a world market for about five computers.
>
> **Thomas J. Watson of IBM**

If we cannot trust the businessmen we will just have to rely on the economists:

> In all likelihood world inflation is over.
>
> **Managing Director of the IMF, 1959**

Energy

M ost likely the universal source of power, then, before the middle of the century, will be the recomposition of water—in other words, we shall get all the power we want by splitting up water into oxygen and hydrogen, and then allowing these gases to recombine, thereby returning to us the energy we have employed in the analysis.

T. Baron Russell, *A Hundred Years Hence*, 1905

Or, better still and more simply, we could obtain power by pumping water up a hill and letting it drive mighty turbines as it comes down again. Phrased in this way, the notion would seem too ridiculous even to be considered. However, this version is not only rather close to Russell's suggestion above but is an almost exact description of one 'perpetual-motion' machine which was granted a British patent:

T REDINNICK'S IMPROVED SELF-DRIVING HYDRAULIC MOTOR consists of a water cistern or reservoir to the bottom of which is connected one or more pipes which pass downwards and are then bent back and pass over or through the walls of the cistern to empty themselves back into the cistern, which empties itself into the pipes as fast as the water is returned into them. The flow of water thus occasioned may be employed for driving machinery.

British Patent 11318/1901

More serious and scientific considerations of energy's future tend to deal with things running out. Herman Kahn and his merry futurologists have prepared an interesting table (it appeared in their *The Next 200 Years*) which covers the various prophecies and realities of American oil production. To summarize:

In 1866 the US Revenue Commission announced optimistically that, when oil production ceased as expected, synthetic fuels could be used instead: in the following eighty-two years thirty-seven billion barrels (BB) were produced without need for synthetics. In

1885 the US Geological Survey pooh-poohed the possibility of oil strikes in California, since which time eight BB have been extracted from that state. In 1891 the Survey said the same about Kansas and Texas: surprise surprise, these states have since produced fourteen BB. In 1908 the Survey forecast doom—a maximum future production of 22.5 BB countrywide ... thirty-five BB have been produced since. By 1914 an official of the US Bureau of Mines was gloomily announcing a mere 5.7 BB total future production: six times this amount has been extracted since. In 1920 the Survey Director had reached the brink of disaster. Peak domestic production had been attained, or nearly so, and foreign oil and synthetics were needed in ever-increasing amounts—but by 1948 American production exceeded consumption, more than quadrupling the 1920 output. In 1931 the Secretary of the Interior moved into the act with stark warnings that as much foreign oil as possible must be imported to conserve domestic supplies: during the next eight years imports were in fact discouraged and fourteen BB unearthed in America. By 1939 the Department of the Interior was issuing frenzied radio broadcasts to the effect that local supplies would dry up in thirteen years. In 1947 the Chief of the Petroleum Division of the US State Department said, doubtless ashen-faced, that American oil was on its last legs: in 1948 they found 4.3 BB, the largest volume of oil discovered in any single year in history. By 1949 new gloom had returned to the Secretary of the Interior, who moaned that the end of the country's oil supply was in sight, whereupon production increased by something like a million barrels daily for five solid years.

All in all, not a fearfully impressive record; though some marks must be awarded for persistence.

Nuclear power was much discussed as oil scare followed oil scare, though several scientists were sceptical:

> On thermodynamical grounds which I can hardly summarize shortly, I do not much believe in the commercial possibility of induced radio-activity.
>
> **J. B. S. Haldane,** *Daedalus,* **1923**

> There is no likelihood man can ever tap the power of the atom. The glib supposition of utilizing atomic energy when our coal has run out is a completely unscientific Utopian dream, a childish bug-a-boo. Nature has introduced a few foolproof devices into the

great majority of elements that constitute the bulk of the world, and they have no energy to give up in the process of disintegration.

Dr Robert Millikan, Nobel Prize winner, 1923

Haldane was a chemist and Millikan had merely worked on such subtleties as the charge on the electron; surely more lightning insight might be expected from the man who first conceived the idea of the atomic nucleus?

There is by no means the same certainty today as a decade ago that the atoms of an element contain hidden sources of energy.

Sir Ernest Rutherford, 1923

And after he had located the hidden sources . . .

The energy produced by the breaking down of the atom is a very poor kind of thing. Anyone who looks for a source of power in the transformation of the atom is talking moonshine.

1933

In 1936 Rutherford was still dismissing nuclear power as 'Utopian', and in the last lecture he gave before his death he added:

The slow neutron is extraordinarily efficient in causing transmutations with a large evolution of energy, but the neutron itself can only be produced by very inefficient processes, so that there appears to be no chance of gaining more energy from the reaction than has to be supplied.

1937

Nor did the cosmic minds of futurologists make the right guesses:

A great deal has been written about the possibilities of producing energy cheaply in large quantities by splitting the atom. It is dangerous to prophesy that anything cannot happen, but at least it seems improbable from our present knowledge of physics. It is possible now to split the atom, but the released energy cannot be utilised usefully and it seems improbable that it ever will. . . . The power of the tides may be made available to produce power on a large scale. If extensively exploited over a long period of time, however, it might result in bringing the moon too close to the earth for safety.

J. P. Lockhart-Mummery, *After Us*, 1936

And politicians were perhaps occasionally a little pessimistic for other reasons:

Eminent science added that in known time several stars have blown up, and wryly concluded that several civilizations have achieved nuclear fusion.

Sir Oswald Mosley, *Broadsheet No. 39,* wherein Mosley is described by A. J. P. Taylor as 'A superb political thinker, the best of our age'

More recently, the politicians have of course run true to form by adopting a (shall we say) variable stance on the nuclear power question. In the 1950s it was said, reputedly in Parliament, that nuclear power would make electricity so cheap that it would not be worth the trouble of installing electricity meters. By the 1970s, the story was that, even if power were totally free, the cost of maintaining the National Grid, the electricity showrooms and (no doubt) the advertising campaigns would mean that no cuts in charges could be made.

Evolution

E ven if we are descended from worms they were
  glorious worms.

J. M. Tyler

When Charles Darwin published his *On the Origin of Species by
Means of Natural Selection* (1859), there was of course a
tremendous fuss—though not at first. At the end of 1858, the year in
which Darwin's and Wallace's papers on the subject had first been
read to the Linnaean Society, its President noted that the year

> has not, indeed, been marked by any of those striking
> discoveries which at once revolutionise, so to speak, the
> department of science in which they occur.

Thomas Bell

Evolution—though not natural selection—had been lurking in the
air for some years, for example in Robert Chambers' book *The
Vestiges of Creation*, which had provoked a swift, authoritative and
subtly reasoned reply:

> I f the book is true, the labours of sober induction are in
>   vain; religion is a lie; human law is a mass of folly, and
> a base injustice; morality is moonshine; our labours for
> the black people of Africa were works of madness; and
> man and woman are only better beasts.

**Adam Sedgwick, Woodwardian Professor of Geology at
Cambridge**

Then Darwin indulged in folly and madness to the extent of
publishing his theory, in which he had been very careful not to state
that men were descended from apes; this omission was swiftly
remedied by his critics, and the hue and cry was on. The first sort of
argument employed was what might be called the Vague
Denunciation, which stated pretty clearly that Darwin was all wet
while maintaining a certain dignified silence as to precisely why.

I have read your book with more pain than pleasure. Parts of it I admired greatly, parts I laughed at till my sides were almost sore: other parts I read with absolute sorrow, because I think them utterly false and grievously mischievous. You have *deserted* ... the true method of induction, and started us in machinery as wild, I think, as Bishop Wilkins's locomotive that was to sail us to the moon...

Adam Sedgwick, letter to Darwin, 1859

Darwin was a master of what may be called scientific *chiaroscuro*, and owes his reputation in no small measure to the judgment with which he kept his meaning dark where a less practised hand would have thrown light on it.

Samuel Butler, 1886

On the matter of man's so-called 'primitive barbarism', or 'Ascent' from savage animal beginnings, testimony is equally decisive. To quote Sir J. W. Dawson [*Origin of the World*]: 'Archaeological remains show no trace of any emergence from barbarism on the part of man, indeed man has gained nothing of moment from the dawn of history. Man's earliest state was his best.'

C. Leopold Clarke, *Evolution and the Break-Up of Christendom*, 1930

Wassman said: 'The whole hypothetical pedigree of man is not supported by a single fossil genus, or a single fossil species.'

Ibid.

[Quoting the *Children's Encyclopaedia*:] 'It seems very hard to believe that the birds with their lovely plumage and their sweet song, came from ugly reptiles.' It does indeed, and in view of the fact that there is no shred of evidence to be found anywhere that any such change has ever taken place, or that any species has ever changed its specific nature, it is still more hard to believe that sane men can state such nonsense as fact.

Ibid.

All that was new in them was false and all that was true in them was old.

Professor Haughton on Darwin's findings

Long after the theory was generally accepted, similar statements were still turning up:

In every text-book on zoology, the evidence in favour of evolution is set forth and nothing against it ... I maintain that if the evidence were more fairly put you would not get half these young men to accept evolution. I was taught it. It took me more than twenty years of work before I discovered it was wrong.

Douglas Dewar, ornithologist and FZS

And of course not all the evolutionists were infallible. One much acclaimed link in humanity's pedigree, of the highest scientific respectability when the following extract was written, turned out to be mere fraud:

Our next illustration (Fig. 11) is of a very celebrated person, the Piltdown Man, *Eoanthropus Dawsoni*, or the Man of the Dawn, so named after his finder, Mr Charles Dawson. We should be very proud of *Eoanthropus*, because he is the first known Englishman. In 1912 men were digging for gravel, and came across a skull which they broke up and threw away; a rather brutal thing to do, and in this case supremely foolish as well. One piece of the skull came into the possession of Mr Dawson, who, recognising its value, at once made search for the remaining portions. Other parts of the skull were found, a lower jaw, and later on a canine tooth. Since 1912 scientific men all over the world have written articles, indulged in friendly controversy, and found out all kinds of things about the Piltdown man.

M. & C. H. B. Quennell, *Everyday Life in the Old Stone Age,*
1921

They found out a thing or two too many in 1953.

Simply saying loudly and continuously that Darwin Is Wrong does not have as much effect as one would like. The next stage of argument went on to say just why the origin of species through natural selection could not be so: it was unthinkable, that was why!

I t is scandalous that children and students should be taught as a proven fact that these ancestors were apes, and should be shown abominable pictures of primitive man as a shaggy ape-like creature with a low forehead, receding chin, bowed back, bent legs. Such science is a disgrace to the spirit of science and a crime against humanity: and the Catholics and Daytonians deserve honour for declining to accept a totally unproved hypothesis.

R. C. Macfie, 1933

N o matter what view he held of the origin of man, the exercise of a little intelligence should convince anyone that none of man's ancestors can have had any of the following characters: (1) A hairy coat to which the young could cling, thus allowing the mother full use of all four limbs for locomotion; (2) Quadrupedal gait; (3) An opposable great toe.

Douglas Dewar, 1944

The way to get a clear perspective on Darwin, you see, was to ignore the facts and just exercise a little intelligence—i.e., allow your prejudices free play. The third type of argument attempts to blast the evolutionary theory by refusing to accept, say, the fossil records:

T he geological record shrieks out the most emphatic refutation of Darwin's doctrine of Natural Selection as the evolutionary power of Nature. . . . Nature most clearly and with no uncertain voice proclaims that, if there has been evolution from lower to higher forms, it has not been slow and gradual processes: for such processes could by no possibility have left the geological record a *tabula rasa* in the matter of intermediate forms.

George Paulin, 1908

It is truly remarkable that palaeontology in no way displays transitional forms between phyla and classes, and, possibly, not even between orders.

Leo S. Berg, 1926

THERE APPEARS TO EXIST NO MECHANISM WHEREBY A NEW TYPE OF ORGANISM CAN ARISE FROM AN EXISTING ONE. This explains why all breeds of dogs, pigeons, etc., are still dogs, pigeons, etc. ... Take a simple one-celled organism, such as an amoeba, which lacks eyes, ears, nose, legs, heart, liver, spleen, pancreas, bones, muscles, nerves, blood, blood-vessels. Shuffle *ad infinitum* the constituent molecules of all the genes that control the organisation of the amoeba, and what can the result be other than a modified amoeba?

Douglas Dewar, 1946

Relatively recent 'creationist' thought has produced a rather splendid refutation of almost anything you care to mention. One of our intrepid researchers attended a lecture given by Dr D. Rosevear, who declared:

The first law of thermodynamics states that matter/energy can neither be created nor destroyed; therefore species cannot create/destroy themselves.

Passing with a shudder over *that* piece of reasoning, we come to a couple of items from long before Darwinism, which might be taken for subtle attempts to undermine it.

We may suppose the whole terrestrial mass to have been taken to pieces and dissolved at the flood, and the strata to have settled down from this promiscuous mass as any earthly sediment from a fluid ... The entire mass of fossiliferous strata contained in the earth's crust was then deposited in a few months.

John Woodward, 1695

Buckland has just noticed in his geological lectures the extraordinary fact, that, among all the hosts of animals which are found and are proved to have existed prior to 6000 years ago, *not one* is there which would be at all serviceable to man; *but* that directly you get within that period, horses, bulls, goats, deer, asses &c. are at once discovered. How strong a presumptive proof from the face of nature of what the Bible asserts to be the case.

John Henry—later Cardinal—Newman, diary entry after attending a lecture by geologist William Buckland, 1821

Almost the most potent argument against poor old outnumbered Darwin is the ever-handy argument from Faith. A mysterious political trend gave the USSR a faith in other evolutionary theories, which gradually hardened through the first half of this century.

I f the tendency towards variation be predetermined, if the production of variations is determined by law, the importance of natural selection is then reduced to zero, as was admirably expressed by Strakov so long ago as 1873: 'Every law which is discovered in the phenomena of variation and heredity leads to the refutation of Darwin's theory. The strength of that theory, its intellectual attractiveness, emphatically consists in the supposition that laws do not exist and the phenomena may be reduced to the play of chance.'

Leo S. Berg, Professor at the University of Leningrad, 1926

What the Soviets inclined to was the teaching of Ivan Michurin, who had swallowed whole the Lamarckian doctrine of inheritance of acquired characteristics—something which, if it worked, would make natural selection unnecessary. Alas, it does not work, and many Soviet geneticists were pointing this out when their masters made a final leap of faith.

The Party, the Government and J. V. Stalin personally, have taken an unflagging interest in the further development of the Michurin teaching.

Trofim D. Lysenko, Report to the Lenin Academy of Agricultural Sciences, 1948

This is the clinching argument. Who needs proof when you have the Party, the Government *and* J. V. Stalin? A few swift purges later, Soviet believers in the foul Darwinian heresy had been relocated to more rewarding tasks such as emptying dustbins, and genetics languished until Lysenko's final lapse from Party favour in 1964.

But the Church also had faith, and continued to have faith. Who, after all, needs proof when you have the Church, the College of Cardinals *and* the Pope? Evolution was being denounced long before Darwin moved into the act:

Wherever we see marks of contrivance, we are led for its cause to an *intelligent* author . . . How will our philosopher get at *vision*, or make an eye? How should the blind animal affect sight, of which blind animals, we know, have neither conception nor desire? Affecting it, by what operation of its will, by what endeavour to see, could it so determine the fluids of its body, as to inchoate the formation of an eye? Or suppose the eye formed, would the perception follow? The same of the other senses . . . No laws, no course, no powers of nature which prevail at present, nor any analogous to these, would give commencement to a new sense . . . Upon the whole: after all the schemes and struggles of a reluctant philosophy, the necessary resort is to a deity. The marks of *design* are too strong to be gotten over. Design must have had a designer. The designer must have been a person. That person is God.

William Paley, DD, *Natural Theology,* **1846**

Yes, indeed. Or was 'that person' William Paley? Another argument from design follows:

Had chance, or nature, as some love to speak, directed the distribution of animals, and they were abandoned to themselves and to the circumstances in which they found themselves in their original station, without any superintending power to guide them, they would not so invariably have fixed themselves in the climates and regions for which they were evidently intended.

The Bridgewater Treatises, **mid-nineteenth century**

Fish, if left to themselves, would have lain on the grass and perished miserably—not knowing any better. The religious denunciation of evolution continues, in muted form, to this day; we merely quote the most recent specimen available at the time of writing.

> S IR—As a 'biblical fundamentalist' and a qualified scientist I stand in awe of Mr Adrian Berry's imagination in his article 'An early family portrait' (February 25). He does, however, seem somewhat lacking in facts—which I have always been led to understand are the basis of science.
>
> He may express wonder that the dawn ape in his 'artist's impression' could have taken such tremendous steps in 30 million years, surely the true reason for wonder is that God created the world in six days.
>
> Letter, *Daily Telegraph*, February 1980

The most potent argument of all against Darwinism, akin to that practised in the USSR once upon a time, is simply to make it illegal. Then, when you are asked 'What about your opponents?', you can respond like the legendary bandit who was invited on his deathbed to forgive his enemies, and explained: 'There are none. I have shot them all'. Observe:

> I t shall be unlawful for any teacher in any of the universities, normals and all other public schools of the state which are supported in whole or in part by the public school funds of the state, to teach any theory that denies the story of the divine creation of man as taught in the Bible, and to teach instead that man has descended from a lower state of animals.
>
> State of Tennessee statute, 1925, repealed 1967

It really is a great pity that the State of Tennessee never got round to doing something equally decisive about the law of gravitation. Had they made gravity a (localized) offence, billions of dollars could have been saved when the time came for the space programme.

The Future

P rediction is very difficult, especially about the future.

Neils Bohr

There are two reliable ways of prophesying the future; the first was practised by touts who would pass amid the crowds at racecourses, whispering into selected ears the names of 'winning' horses. The important part of their method was to give as a winner (though not at the same time) the name of every horse running; an excellent memory was also needed so that you could revisit each person to whom you had prophesied the actual winner, and perhaps collect some reward. The other method, in racecourse terms, is simply to back every favourite for a place: this is the system used by such thinkers as Herman Kahn and the Hudson Institute in their calculation of 'surprise-free' futures. Clive James once produced an excellent summary of Kahn's golden rule: it predicts that in 'fivetenfifteentwennytwennyfiveyearsfromnow' anything now happening will still be happening but more so—unless something stops it. (The second law, he added, states that the fee for being told the first will be very large.) In just such a way do stock-market analysts infallibly predict that the market will get better some time, and slump some other time; the numerologist Vincent Lopez made much of his prediction that World War II would end one day. A third method, employed by Nostradamus, the sixteenth-century astrologer, is to make such an incomprehensible prediction that only after the event can anyone decide what you were predicting.

Less successful methods assume that the future can be exactly measured by the past and present:

I n all probability the next doubling of the people of England will be in about six hundred years to come, or by the year of our Lord 2300, at which time it will have eleven millions of people. The next doubling after that will be, in all probability, in less than twelve or thirteen hundred years, or by the year of our Lord 3500 or 3600. At which time the Kingdom will have 22 millions of souls ... in case the world should last so long.

Gregory King, *Observations on the State of England*, 1696

One of the most effective prophecies against London
... was that given out in the spring of 1750, after a
slight shock of an earthquake was felt in London, and it
was prophesied that another should occur which would
destroy the town and all its inhabitants. All the roads
were thronged with persons flying to the country a day
or two before the threatened event ...

Isaac Disraeli, *Curiosities of Literature*, 1791–3

When we get piled upon one another in large cities,
we shall become as corrupt as in Europe, and go to
eating one another as they do there.

Thomas Jefferson, 1787

Executions are so much a part of British history that it
is almost impossible for many excellent people to
think of the future without them.

Viscount Templewood, *In the Shadow of the Gallows*, 1951

Or perhaps one can decide the future once and for all by sheer will-
power (of course, it does help to be a lunatic):

By this revolution the German way of life is definitely
settled for the next thousand years.

Adolf Hitler, 1934

The day of individual happiness has passed.

Ibid.

A new age of magic interpretation of the world is
coming, of interpretation in terms of the will and not
of the intelligence. There is no such thing as truth, either
in the moral or the scientific sense.

Ibid.

Hitler also made some more specific prophecies, whose validity you
must judge for yourselves.

In a hundred years, our language will be the language
of Europe.

***Table Talk*, 1941**

E ngland and America will one day have a war with one another, which will be waged with the greatest hatred imaginable. One of the two countries will have to disappear.

Ibid.

T he Japanese are occupying all the islands, one after another. They will get hold of Australia, too. The White Race will disappear from those regions.

Ibid.

T he beauties of the Crimea, which we shall make accessible by means of an autobahn—for us Germans, that will be our Riviera.

Ibid.

How, we ask, should we prepare for this glorious future?

T he essential thing for the future is to have lots of children. Everybody should be persuaded that the family's life is assured only when it has upwards of four children—I should even say, four sons.

Ibid.

Less single-minded prophets, perhaps inspired by H. G. Wells' fictional utopias, plumped for a wide spectrum of not always consistent predictions—

S uch a wasteful food as animal flesh cannot survive: and even apart from the moral necessity which will compel mankind, for its own preservation, to abandon the use of alcohol, the direct and indirect wastefulness of alcohol will make it impossible for beverages containing it to be tolerated. Very likely tobacco will follow it.

T. Baron Russell, *A Hundred Years Hence,* **1905**

... modern rooms, equally with those of all time, seem to have been constructed so as to make it as difficult as possible to keep them clean. Square corners and rectangular junctions of wall and floor, wall and ceiling, will certainly before long be replaced everywhere by curves.

Ibid.

D emocracy will be dead by 1950.

John Langdon-Davies, *A Short History of the Future*, **1936**

T here will be no war in western Europe for the next five years [from 1935].

Ibid.

B y 1960 work will be limited to three hours a day.

Ibid.

A bundant new raw materials will [by 1960] make food, clothing and other necessities universally obtainable.

Ibid.

B y 1975 parents will have ceased to bring up their children in private family units.

Ibid.

B y 1975 sexual feeling and marriage will have nothing to do with each other.

Ibid.

C rime will be considered a disease after 1985 and will cease to exist by AD2000.

Ibid.

It should be mentioned that Langdon-Davies's are no mere casual predictions: no indeed! They are COSMIC JUDGEMENTS, and as such were printed in HUGE BLOCK CAPITALS. The last, of course, has a special charm in that it has not yet failed to come about, but we note that crime is still handled by the courts rather than the

National Health Service—and still appears to be a growth industry with expansion potential for the next twenty years. But such optimism is tempting.

Our star turn for this chapter is Winwood Reade, author of *The Martyrdom of Man* (1872)—a book which so impressed Sir Arthur Conan Doyle that he plugged it in a Sherlock Holmes story. Reade believed in determinism:

> When we have ascertained, by means of science, the method of Nature's operations, we shall be able to take her place and to perform them for ourselves. When we understand the laws which regulate the complex phenomena of life we shall be able to predict the future as we are already able to predict comets and eclipses and the planetary movements.

Thus, and in defiance of Heisenberg's Uncertainty Principle which later made determinism an uncertain (as it were) philosophy, he went on to predict,

> Three inventions which perhaps may be long delayed, but which possibly are near at hand, will give to this overcrowded island the prosperous conditions of the United States. The first is the discovery of a motive force which will take the place of steam, with its cumbrous fuel of oil or coal; the second, the invention of aerial locomotion which will transport labour at a trifling cost of money and of time to any part of the planet, and which by annihilating distance will speedily extinguish national distinctions; the third, the manufacture of flesh and flour from the elements by a chemical process in the laboratory, similar to that which is now performed within the bodies of animals and plants. Food will then be manufactured in unlimited quantities at a trifling expense, and our enlightened posterity will look back upon us who eat oxen and sheep just as we look back upon cannibals. Hunger and starvation will then be unknown, and the best part of human life will no longer be wasted in the tedious process of cultivating the fields. Population will mightily increase, and the earth will be a garden. Governments will be conducted with the quietude and regularity of club committees. The interest which is now

felt in politics will be transferred to science; the latest news from the laboratory of the chemist or the observatory of the astronomer or the experimenting room of the biologist will be eagerly discussed. Poetry and the fine arts will take that place in the heart which religion now holds. Luxuries will be cheapened and made common to all; none will be rich and none poor. Not only will man subdue the forces of evil that are without; he will also subdue those that are within. He will repress the base instincts and propensities which he has inherited from the animals below; he will obey the laws that are written on his heart; he will worship the divinity within him. As our conscience forbids us to commit actions which the conscience of the savage allows, so the moral sense of our successors will stigmatise as crimes those offences against the intellect which are sanctioned by ourselves. Idleness and stupidity will be regarded with abhorrence. Women will become the companions of men and the tutors of their children. The whole world will be united by the same sentiment which united the primeval clan, and which made its members think, feel and act as one. Men will look upon this star as their fatherland; its progress will be their ambition, the gratitude of others their reward. These bodies which now we wear belong to the lower animals; our minds have already outgrown them; already we look upon them with contempt. A time will come when science will transform them by means which we cannot conjecture, and which, even if explained to us, we could not now understand, just as the savage cannot understand electricity, magnetism, or steam. Disease will be extirpated; the causes of decay will be removed; immortality will be invented. And then, the earth being small, mankind will migrate into space, and will cross the airless Saharas which separate planet from planet and sun from sun. The earth will become a Holy Land which will be visited by pilgrims from all the quarters of the universe. Finally, men will master the forces of Nature; they will become themselves architects of systems, manufacturers of worlds.

Man then will be perfect . . .

It is embarrassing to note that all three of Reade's inventions have been available for some while—internal combustion engines, air travel, synthetic foods—yet unaccountably we have failed to become perfect.

Specific prophecies, as explained above, are hard to come by in these shifty times, so it is with delight that we record the warning of an American gentleman called Creswell who says that some city in the USA will be destroyed by poison gas in 1981. It was merciful of him not to specify the city and date, otherwise people might have injured themselves in the rush as they thronged the roads while 'flying to the country a day or two before the event'.

Two final views of the future, yet to be disproved:

> In a hundred years the unification of the human race will be complete. The earth and the fulness thereof will be under the full mastery of man. All animal, vegetable and bacterial life will be kept within strict bounds in the interests of humanity. The earth will be under one government, and one language will be written and understood, or even spoken, all over the globe. There will still be different races and perhaps allied nations, but travel and commerce will be freed and unfettered, and calamities will be alleviated and dangers met by the united forces of all mankind.
>
> **E. E. Fournier d'Albe, *Quo Vadimus?*, 1925**

Only forty-five years left and quite a way to go, we would say.

> '. . . The final certificate does not so much signify a good preparation in general culture but guarantees that the student has a profession at his fingertips—automation, telecontrolled mining, or atomic-power-station operator, electronic computer mechanic, etc.'
>
> 'The main professions of the twenty-first century,' one of us cried.
>
> **M. Vassiliev & S. Gouschev, *Life in the Twenty-First Century*, chapter on 'The School of the Future', 1960**

'Indeed?' both of us cried.

Inventions

The advancement of the art [of invention] from year to year ... seems to presage the arrival of that period when further improvement must end.

Henry L. Ellsworth, US Commissioner of Patents, 1844

We suppose that at just about any period of history one can imagine, the average dim-witted official will have doubted that anything new can be produced: the attitude cropped up again in 1899, when the Director of the US Patent Office urged President McKinley to abolish the Office, and even the post of Director, since:

Everything that can be invented has been invented.

Or, moving back well over two millennia:

The thing that hath been, it is that which shall be; and that which is done is that which shall be done: and there is no new thing under the sun.

Ecclesiastes i, 9

Moreover, inventors just have no class at all:

In my own time there have been inventions of this sort, transparent windows, tubes for diffusing warmth equally through all parts of a building, short-hand, which has been carried to such a pitch of perfection that a writer can keep pace with the most rapid speaker. But the inventing of such things is drudgery for the lowest slaves; philosophy lies deeper ...

Lucius Annaeus Seneca (4BC–AD65)

History is littered with the bones of inventors who were roundly snubbed for inventing the right things; for example, gas lamps:

There is a young madman proposing to light the streets of London—with what do you suppose— with smoke!

Sir Walter Scott, 1810

Inventing the computer in the nineteenth century, as Charles Babbage did, was also incautious:

T his extraordinary monument of theoretical genius accordingly remains, and doubtless will for ever remain, a theoretical possibility.

Biographer of Charles Babbage, twelve years after his death in 1871

Around 1878, when Edison was developing his incandescent lamp, a British Parliamentary Committee was established to decide whether such new-fangled nonsense could ever be relevant to Britain. In general the idea was thought

... good enough for our transatlantic friends ... but unworthy of the attention of practical or scientific men.

The committee also produced the ringing denunciation:

S ub-division of the electric light is an absolute *ignis fatuus*.

Sir William Preece, Engineer-in-Chief of the Post Office

When 'our transatlantic friends' had seen Edison's first demonstration, there were such comments as:

E veryone acquainted with the subject will recognize it as a conspicuous failure.

Henry Morton, President of the Stevens Institute of Technology

Edison himself was mightily annoyed when even younger inventors suggested the electrical distribution system used today: he favoured low voltages and direct current, which worked quite well but tended to melt the supply cables.

T here is no plea which will justify the use of high-tension and alternating currents, either in a scientific or a commercial sense. They are employed solely to reduce investment in copper wire and real estate.

My personal desire would be to prohibit entirely the use of alternating currents. They are unnecessary as they are dangerous . . . I can therefore see no justification for the introduction of a system which has no element of permanency and every element of danger to life and property.

I have always consistently opposed high-tension and alternating systems of electric lighting, not only on account of danger, but because of their general unreliability and unsuitability for any general system of distribution.

Thomas Alva Edison, 1889

The telephone fared even worse, initially. Alexander Bell offered to sell the invention outright to a privately owned telegraph company for $100,000: the offer was declined. Eventually, when telephones were made available for business use, they were rejected by several office managers as unnecessary—how, after all, was it possible to improve upon the existing system of messenger boys?

A nother improvement . . . was that we built our gas chambers to accommodate two thousand people at one time.

Rudolf Hess

The new improved gas chamber was probably close to the ultimate in *undesirable* inventions; patent listings swarm with far more charming and far less useful items, like Krimer and Andrew's Improved Moustache Guards for Drinking Purposes (British Patent 5723/1901) or Turnbull's Self-Emptying Spittoon for the Floors of Railway Carriages (8429/1901). The nineteenth century saw some more practical items, whether or not they actually worked—for example, Dr Sanden's Electric Belt:

I nvented Solely for the Cure of All Weaknesses of Men. We positively guarantee it to cure all forms of Nervous Debility, Impotency, Spermatorrhea, Night Emissions, Shrunken Parts, Nervousness, Forgetfulness, Confusion of Ideas, Languor, Dyspepsia, Lame Back, Rheumatism, Kidney and Bladder Complaint, and the many evils resulting from secret habits in youth or passionate excesses in maturer years. We guarantee our patent improved Electric Suspensory to Enlarge Shrunken or Undeveloped Organs, or no pay.

Just think, 'torturers' in South America and elsewhere who merrily attach electrodes to the testicles may in fact be curing all the weaknesses of men listed above. (These politically-minded electricians are especially good at eradicating Confusion of Ideas.)

Britain is not alone: numerous unlikely American patents exist. Dating from 1872 is the Quinby flying apparatus, to be worn by one person and resembling the wings of a bat (except for the stirrups):

It is intended to start from the ground. In order to make a beginning one foot is disengaged from the stirrup when—by raising the other foot and pushing the hands upward and forward as in swimming—the wings are raised. Then, by suddenly depressing the wings, by means of the elevated leg, the former are intended to elevate the body by their action on the air. This alternate elevation and depression of the wings is continued as long as flight is desired. After rising from the ground the other foot may be inserted in its stirrup and both legs used. The actions are intended to be natural, resembling those of swimming in water.

Watson F. Quinby

From Mr Quinby's failure to get off the ground and into the record books we can only speculate that he was, perhaps, a nonswimmer. But there were many other hopefuls: in 1887 a US patent was granted to a Frenchman, M. Wulff, for a balloon propelled by birds—eagles, vultures or condors would do quite well, though no instructions for obtaining such were included. The birds are firmly attached by 'corsets or harnesses' to an upper platform of the balloon. The inventor says:

It may be observed that the birds have only to fly, the direction of their flight being changed by the conductor quite independently of their own will.

Flying with the help of birds was by no means a new idea: it had been mooted numerous times since its mythological origins; fictional voyages to the Moon had been accomplished that way; even the towing of a balloon had been seriously suggested just over a century earlier. Obviously M. Wulff was the first with sufficient cheek to patent the idea.

Even by the time of World War I the US Patent Office was not sophisticated enough to divide the wheat from the chaff; hence the 1915 patent awarded to the idea of arming a ship with powerful electromagnets, so that lurking enemy submarines (or perhaps even the buttons on one's own uniform jacket) would be attracted and electrified, causing widespread havoc, though exactly how wide a spread is not specified.

We must acknowledge our gratitude to Stacy V. Jones, whose book *Inventions Necessity is Not the Mother Of* was responsible for rescuing the last three (and many other) early US patents from undeserved oblivion.

Numerous perpetual motion machines have also been patented, one of the best being described in our chapter on Energy. The US Patent Office started demanding working models as from 1911, and the British Patent Office began objecting to inventions 'contrary to well-established natural laws' in 1932. One of the simplest perpetual-motion devices:

K*wiatkowski and Stefanski's Improved Water Power Engine* is operated by a waterwheel which, via cranks and lazy tongs, pumps water to itself.

British Patent 5723/1904

Several books could be filled with strange patents; several have. (The British Patents mentioned here are lifted from Rodney Dale and Joan Gray's *Edwardian Inventions*, 1979.) This final item is perhaps the one which most made us smite our foreheads and cry, 'Why didn't we think of that?' ...

P*ugh's Method of Preventing and Curing Consumption and other Kindred Wasting Diseases* follows the lines laid down by the highest medical and most competent physiological authorities: the best known treatment is the inhalation of pure dry air and the employment of medicines has not been, and cannot be, efficacious. All scientific investigations point to the certainty that in the strata of the atmosphere some thousands of feet above the earth are to be found the ideal conditions for the treatment of such complaints. Recent experiments by leading scientists have demonstrated that patients who have been taken up in balloons to a height of 8,000 feet have shown astonishing improvements in their health, and it has also been proved that rarefied air at even 6,000 feet has a totally different effect to mountain air of much higher altitudes. This apparatus accordingly provides a means of providing such pure, life-giving air, free from noxious microbes, from the upper atmosphere to supply the wants of sufferers on the ground. It comes through a tube supported by hydrogen balloons of aluminium at quarter-mile intervals, the air tube being of tempered aluminium sections, corrugated and soldered together and terminating in a lofty-ceilinged building or chamber in which the patients are to be treated. One or two thousand patients at a time may be treated in this way.

British Patent 26500/1904

But if only Pugh had taken the idea further! Increase the altitude to a few thousand miles and the pipeline—now dangling from a satellite—will open into the vacuum of space. No more expensive vacuum pumps or vacuum cleaners—this extended pipeline would make endless supplies of hard vacuum available on tap.

Yes, yes, we must patent this.

Literature

I see no point in reading.

Louis XIV

The attitude of King Louis is rare in these days when everyone knows that reading books enables one to pass examinations, leap high buildings, outdistance speeding trains and even resist the onslaught of *The Times* crossword . . . though sometimes we pause, study the bestseller lists and privately think that Louis had a point after all. Literature *is* one of the most ancient sources of controversy. It was very long ago that an enthusiastic censor burned the great library at Alexandria, supposedly because each of the books must either (a) agree with the Koran and thus be superfluous or (b) disagree with it and thus be blasphemous. Libraries still earlier have been recorded:

The Irish antiquities mention *public libraries* that were before the flood; and Paul Christian Ilker, with profounder erudition, has given an exact catalogue of *Adam's*.

Isaac Disraeli, *Curiosities of Literature,* **1791–3**

Eve presumably left it to her husband to maintain the family library, since in older days women's involvement in literature was not thought terribly nice:

A woman who writes commits two sins: she increases the number of books and decreases the number of women.

Jean Baptiste Alphonse Karr

This, incidentally, is reminiscent of Jorge Luis Borges's heresiarch of Uqbar—from his story 'Tlön, Uqbar, Orbis Tertius'—who said that mirrors and copulation were abominable since they both multiplied the number of men.

Traditionally women have often concealed their names in order to pass in the wicked male-chauvinist-pig world of literature, thus confounding the occasional critic, even in more recent times.

I t has been suggested that Tiptree is female, a theory I find absurd, for there is to me something ineluctably masculine about Tiptree's writing. I don't think the novels of Jane Austen could have been written by a man nor the stories of Ernest Hemingway by a woman, and in the same way I believe the author of the James Tiptree stories is male.

Robert Silverberg, introduction to *Warm Worlds and Otherwise* by James Tiptree Jr, 1975

At the beginning of 1977 James Tiptree Jr was revealed as Alice Sheldon, a sixty-one-year-old spinster.

Although sometimes the massed critical battalions fall on some work which later is 'rehabilitated'—Ibsen's plays are an example, opening to a barrage of Press notices about open drains, loathsome sores, garbage, offal, etc.—the 'mistaken' denunciation is generally an individual, subjective matter like the following:

I would rather put a phial of prussic acid into the hands of a healthy boy or girl than the book in question.

James Douglas, review of Radclyffe Hall's *The Well of Loneliness*

T he telephone directory is, because of its rigorous selection and repression, a work of art compared to the wastepaper basket. And [James Joyce's] *Ulysses* is a wastepaper basket.

Gerald Gould, *The English Novel of Today*, 1924

M y God, what a clumsy *olla putrida* James Joyce is! Nothing but old fags and cabbage-stumps of quotations from the Bible and the rest, stewed in the juice of deliberate, journalistic dirty-mindedness.

D. H. Lawrence

Lawrence, it can be seen, believed his own sex scenes to be very much purer and nicer than those of that horrid intellectual Joyce. He had a pure mind, did Lawrence. So, it seems, did Henry James.

H enry James had a mind so fine that no idea could violate it.

T. S. Eliot

If Mr Eliot had been pleased to write in demotic English, *The Waste Land* might not have been, as it is to all but anthropologists and literati, so much waste-paper.

Manchester Guardian critic

Dr Donne's verses are like the peace of God; they pass all understanding.

James I

Fricassee of dead dog.

Thomas Carlyle, of Keats' collected works

We could go on for page after page listing such mayhem amongst (perhaps) relatively small fry. But surely no one would be so misguided as to denounce, say, Shakespeare?

Shakespeare's comedies are altogether non-acceptable to America and Democracy.

Walt Whitman

With the single exception of Homer, there is no eminent writer, not even Sir Walter Scott, whom I can despise so entirely as I despise Shakespeare when I measure my mind against his . . . It would positively be a relief to dig him up and throw stones at him.

George Bernard Shaw

I think Shakespeare is shit. Absolute shit! He may have been a genius for his time, but I just can't relate to that stuff. 'Thee' and 'thou'—the guy sounds like a faggot. Captain America is classic because he's more enter-taining. If you counted the number of people who read Shakespeare, you'd be very disappointed.

Gene Simmons, of the rock group Kiss

To be fair, one of these critics was reacting against the excessive Victorian admiration of Shakespeare and trying to restore a sense of proportion, while another, we fear, may suffer from an inability to read even Captain America comics without moving his lips. (To avoid the risk of libel suits we do not specify which person we refer to in each case.) As was just said, Shakespeare was ridiculously adored in the last century, but this did not prevent actor-managers from rearranging plays to suit themselves, while their maiden aunts took well-sharpened scissors to the 'unsuitable' parts:

> G entlemen, welcome! ladies that have their toes
> Unplagu'd with corns will have a bout with you—
> Ah ha! my mistresses! which of you all
> Will now deny to dance? she that makes dainty
> She, I'll swear hath corns.

This shocking passage from *Romeo and Juliet* was cut out in Miss Rosa Baughan's 1863 edition, thus concealing the hideous truth about corns from the countless young girls at whom this version was aimed. Perhaps the 'editor' who went furthest was Thomas Bulfinch (of *Mythology* fame), who in 1865 published his super-bowdlerized Shakespeare, wherein Lady Macbeth cries:

> O ut, crimson spot!

Of course, this tampering went right across the board. In 1898 a novel by one T. Mullett Ellis was refused distribution because a bookshop manager declared that he 'objected to the title, and that he would not allow it to be exposed upon the railway bookstalls for that reason'. The objectionable title was *God is Love*.

A censored *Canterbury Tales* was edited by Leigh Hunt, who could not stomach the observation 'Thy breath full sour stinketh', and substituted:

> ... and sure I am
> Thy breath resembleth not sweet marjoram.

Even the Bible, the unalterable word of God, was altered in countless ways to gloss over the regrettable fact that the old Jews had indulged in a certain amount of begetting. At least one edition omitted the *Song of Solomon* altogether, except for the title; others buried this and various other parts considered dangerously erotic in a maze of 'programmed reading' recommendations, small print, appendices and other instruments of concealment. Noah Webster of *Webster's Dictionary* fame (who, incidentally, forced the obsolete past participle 'gotten' on America, simply because he felt the correct English 'got' sounded inadequately genteel) had a go at the Bible's text: when Job complained,

> W hy died I not from the womb? why did I not give up
> the ghost when I came out of the belly?

Webster supplied him with the far snappier utterance,

W hy did I not expire at the time of my birth?

William Alexander, in 1828, also fiddled with the Bible. Where in Leviticus it says that no one can be a priest if he 'hath his stones broken' or 'crushed testicles' (depending on whether you read the King James or Standard versions) Alexander tastefully offered 'who hath a rupture'.

The Bible was a favourite place for printers' errors. Here are some celebrated ones, most of which (in more pious ages) brought down the wrath of God on to the luckless printers in the form of crippling fines:

T hou shalt commit adultery.

1631

T he fool hath said in his heart there is a God. . . .
Know ye not that the unrighteous shall inherit the Kingdom of God?

1653

S in on more.

1716—originally 'sin no more'

It is not surprising that some providential finger changed the word 'princes' in a 1702 edition, to give:

P rinters have persecuted me without a cause.

Ignorance as well as accident must be responsible for many literary slips. James Thurber noted that in 1865, while *Punch* was running its usual awful jokes and all the Tenniel drawings that everyone has now forgotten, *Alice in Wonderland* was published and totally ignored by them. Ah well, this was just a children's book—like *The House at Pooh Corner*, which in 1928 was given the works by no less a wit than Dorothy Parker, in her 'Constant Reader' column for *The New Yorker*.

A nd it is that word 'hummy', my darlings, that marks the first place in *The House at Pooh Corner* at which Tonstant Weader Fwowed Up.

Judging from the numbers of contemporary editions, Milne does seem to be lasting a bit better.

Then we have:

The vigorous school of science fiction writers has produced no really outstanding work since the 1930s.

Pear's Cyclopaedia, **article on 'The Contemporary Novel',**
83rd edition, 1974

Since the 1930s were mostly notable for the abysmal depths of pulp-magazine science fiction, while the non-outstanding items written since then include one or two quite well-known books like *Nineteen Eighty-four*, we are on the whole at a loss for words. This was a state never suffered from by Dr Johnson, who has a final word to say on a book we could have sworn we saw in print only the other day—but obviously this was mere optical illusion, since:

Nothing odd will do long. *Tristram Shandy* did not last.

Samuel Johnson, 1776

Medicine

The sound of the flute will cure epilepsy, and a sciatic gout.

Theophrastus (c. 370–285BC)

Early medicine was very strong on theory, usually vaguely religious theories. One horror story will do as an illustration.

In the twelfth century, an Arab doctor, Thabit, was asked to look after some European settlers in the East. He described his experiences:

They took me to see a knight who had an abscess on his leg, and a woman with consumption. I applied a poultice to the leg, and the abscess opened and began to heal. I prescribed a cleansing and refreshing diet for the woman. Then there appeared a Frankish [European] doctor, who said: 'This man has no idea how to cure these people!' He turned to the knight and said: 'Which would you prefer, to live with one leg or to die with two?' When the knight replied that he would prefer to live with one leg, he sent for a strong man and a sharp axe. They arrived, and I stood by to watch. The doctor supported the leg on a block of wood and said to the man: 'Strike a mighty blow, and cut cleanly!' And there, before my eyes, the fellow struck the knight one blow, and then another, for the first had not finished the job. The marrow spurted out of the leg, and the patient died instantaneously. Then the doctor examined the woman and said: 'She has a devil in her head who is in love with her. Cut her hair off!' This was done, and she went back to eating her usual Frankish food, garlic and mustard, which made her illness worse. 'The devil has got into her brain,' pronounced the doctor. He took a razor and cut a cross on her head, and removed the skull so that the inside of the brain was laid bare. This he rubbed with salt; the woman died instantly. At this juncture I asked whether they had any further need of me, and as they had none I came away, having learnt things about medical methods that I never knew before.

The religious viewpoint constantly denied the existence of such things as germs, an attitude which persisted for many centuries:

All diseases of Christians are to be ascribed to demons.

St Augustine (354–430)

Possibly religion is hazardous to your health; possibly atheists and followers of other faiths are privileged to catch their germs from angels.

If we are afflicted with smallpox, it is because we had a carnival last winter, feasting the flesh, which has offended the Lord.

Catholic priest in Montreal, 1885

This explains why the carnival-loving Catholic community—who incidentally had refused vaccination as 'bidding defiance to Heaven itself, even to the will of God'—caught smallpox while Protestants and even atheists did not. And while on the subject of smallpox:

The medical broadcasters and writers of leading articles still keep repeating like parrots that vaccination abolished smallpox, though vaccinia is now killing more children than smallpox.

George Bernard Shaw, *Everybody's Political What's What*, 1944

(At the time of writing, smallpox is extinct outside the laboratory.)

Dr Johnson dismissed the germ theory of St Kilda's (see below) as an old wives' tale, while an ingenious alternative theory soon appeared:

[Johnson] said, 'Macaulay, who writes the account of St Kilda, set out with a prejudice against prejudices, and wanted to be a smart modern thinker; and yet he affirms for a truth, that when a ship arrives there, all the inhabitants are seized with a cold.'

... The late Reverend Mr Christian, of Docking— after ruminating a little, 'The cause (says he), is a natural one. The situation of St Kilda renders a North-East Wind indispensibly necessary before a stranger can land. The wind, not the stranger, causes an epidemic cold.'

Boswell, *Life of Johnson*, Spring 1768 entries

Boswell does mention a Dr John Campbell who came closer, believing colds to be spread *via* 'effluvia from human bodies': later this viewpoint was to be distorted by cranks who insisted that microbes were not the prime cause of disease, but were produced by the human body as a reaction to disease. Diseases, in other words, cause germs. George Bernard Shaw held this opinion, and others more dubious:

The simplest way to kill most microbes is to throw them into an open street or river and let the sun shine on them, which explains that when great cities have recklessly thrown all their sewage into the open river the water has sometimes been cleaner twenty miles below the city than thirty miles above it ... All through Europe people are adjured, by public notices and even under legal penalties, not to throw their microbes into the sunshine, but to collect them carefully in a handkerchief ...

George Bernard Shaw, preface to *The Doctor's Dilemma*, 1911

In the first frenzy of microbe killing, surgical instruments were dipped in carbolic oil ... Microbes are so fond of carbolic oil that they swarm in it.

Ibid.

Fortunately in a world of such lurking perils, where even disinfectant bottles swarm with sinister microbes, there is a last-ditch solution:

There are numerous diseases which can be not merely cured, but ultimately abolished when we have once discovered how to use oxygen adequately. ... Liquefied oxygen will no doubt be our sole disinfectant. It will also replace the poisonous, noisome and destructive bleaching agents used today.

T. Baron Russell, *A Hundred Years Hence*, 1905

And, if even that fails, Bishop Berkeley, in the eighteenth century, went overboard about the virtues of a dismal-sounding infusion of wood-tar in cold water:

It is good not only in fevers, diseases of the lungs, cancer, scrofula, throat diseases, apoplexies, chronic diseases of all kinds, but also as a general drink for infants.

Bishop Berkeley, *Further Thoughts on Tar-Water*, 1752.

The stuff was popular, *viz.* Horace Walpole's *Letters* for 1744:

A man came into an apothecary's shop the other day. 'Do you sell tar-water?' 'Tar-water!' replied the apothecary, 'why, I sell nothing else!'

That is the great advantage of panaceas: they do reduce the number of remedies an apothecary/chemist needs to keep in stock. With more commercial acumen Bishop Berkeley could, perhaps, have made his tar-water by a secret formula and invented numerous weird disorders which it alone would cure. This imaginative leap was made by the lady whose vast medicinal empire inspired the 1968 pop song 'Lily the Pink':

Besides these nervous strains, there is what might be called nerve-starvation. In such cases the blood is impoverished, and fails to feed the nerves properly, the thousands of nerve threads in the body shrivel and waste, and the pain they give is really a cry of hunger. The tonic properties of Lydia E. Pinkham's Vegetable Compound cause it to relieve depression of the nerves. If the nerves are worn out from the strain on the nerve centres, caused by local female disorders, Lydia E. Pinkham's Vegetable Compound will, by effecting a cure of these disorders, remove the cause of nerve troubles ...

Lydia E. Pinkham's *Private Text-Book upon Ailments
Peculiar to Women*

I ndigestion is very closely connected with diseases and ailments of the female organs.

Ibid.

The Vegetable Compound is cited as curing: menstrual pains, all conceivable menstrual problems, derangement of the generative organs, change-of-life ills, liability of miscarriage, exhaustion during pregnancy, 'failing to get along right in any way', falling of the womb, inflammation of the womb, discharge from the womb, most tumours, inflamed ovaries, hysteria, nerve-starvation, headaches, neuralgia, melancholy, incipient insanity, anaemia ('Science has discovered no treatment for this serious ailment to compare with Lydia E. Pinkham's Vegetable Compound'), indigestion, dyspepsia, bad breath, flatulence, bladder troubles, colds, kidney diseases, dropsy, rheumatism and obesity. When supplemented with Lydia E. Pinkham's Blood Purifier, Liver Pills and Sanative Wash, there is nothing save major amputation which the Compound will not cure. No wonder the big drug companies suppressed it.

Several more modern, and doubtless equally effective, medical theories are cited in John Sladek's comprehensive guide to strange beliefs, *The New Apocrypha*:

N o illness is more simple to cure than cancer (this also applies to mental diseases and heart trouble) through a return to the most elementary natural eating and drinking: Diet No. 7.

George Ohsawa, *Zen Macrobiotics*, 1965

(Diet No. 7 consisted of whole-grain cereal and minimal liquids— nothing else. Scurvy, anyone?)

H itler was a typical example of sugar addiction relating to a tendency towards crime ... The evidence is there. There can be no question about it. Hitler must have suffered from low blood sugar due to an overconsumption of sugar.

Jerome Irving Rodale, *Natural Health, Sugar and the Criminal Mind*, 1968

Luckily there is one herbal remedy whose power might counteract even the murderous ravages of sugar:

The power of tobacco to sustain the system, to keep up nutrition, to maintain and increase the weight, to brace against severe exertion, and to replace ordinary food, is a matter of daily and hourly demonstration.

George Black, *The Doctor at Home,* *c.*1898

Overlapping now into the field of psychiatry, we have the strange and all-embracing views of L. Ron Hubbard, 'inventor' of scientology. Unconsciousness, for example, does not really exist.

If you care to make the experiment you can take a man, render him 'unconscious', hurt him and give him information. By dianetic technique, no matter what information you gave him it can be recovered. This experiment should not be carelessly conducted because *you might also render him insane.*

L. Ron Hubbard, *Dianetics,* **1951**

Say nothing and make no sound around an 'unconscious' or injured person. To speak, no matter what is said, is to threaten his sanity.

Ibid.

'Toothache' is normally psycho-somatic. Organic illnesses enough to fill several catalogues are psycho-somatic.

Ibid.

After this, even the hearty remarks of politicians confronted with medical matters seem relatively mild:

Many Britons a hundred years ago were bursting with good health, and the remarkable thing was that they knew nothing of vitamins.

Lord Horder

No woman should be kept on the Pill for 20 years until, in fact, a sufficient number have been kept on the Pill for 20 years.

Sir Alan Sterling Parks, 1970

I n the opinion of leading medical experts, milk given without medical supervision can do positive harm.

Alderman Arthur Barret, *c.*1970

Our diagnoses in these last three cases are (a) inability to realize that vitamins existed even before they were discovered, (b) total aphasia, and (c) morbid desire to abolish free milk at state schools.

Music

Most people are acoustically deaf and don't even notice the acoustic pollution of the world.

Karlheinz Stockhausen, 1971

Could this notoriously avant-garde composer be an example of the pot calling the kettle black? In fact, most people (not considering themselves to be 'most people') would probably think of current trends in popular music and agree with Stockhausen.

But it has always been the fate of new styles of music to be condemned vigorously at first. Many of the most highly respected classical composers were attacked—particularly by backward-looking critics—for some or all of their work, and it has taken a generation or a century for their true worth to be realized.

I liked your opera. I think I will put it to music.

Beethoven to a fellow composer

Is Wagner a human being at all? Is he not rather a disease? He contaminates everything he touches—he has made music sick, I postulate this viewpoint: Wagner's art is diseased.

Friedrich Nietzsche, *Der Fall Wagner*

Wagner is the Puccini of music.

J. B. Morton

There are similar instances in the field of popular music, too. For example, that perennial favourite, 'Somewhere Over the Rainbow', was very nearly cut out of the musical film *The Wizard of Oz*. What a loss to the world that would have been! And, worse, the part which Judy Garland made so famous (and which made her so famous) was almost given to Shirley Temple.

When rock and roll was young it, too, had to suffer the indignities of harsh, unthinking criticism:

R ock 'n' roll is phony and false, and sung, written and played for the most part by cretinous goons.

Frank Sinatra, 1957

Possibly he has since regretted those hasty words. But such hastiness has continued, even in those who should know better. For example, the verdict of the Beatles' first record audition in London was:

T hese boys won't make it. Four-groups are out. Go back to Liverpool, Mr Epstein, you have a good business there.

If it had not been for the Beatles' Liverpool sense of humour and their plucky determination to succeed despite this early setback, their talents might forever have been lost to the world. As one of their number, the lovable Ringo Starr, said in humble acknowledgement of the extent to which the Beatles were influenced by an understanding of classical music:

I love Beethoven, especially the poems.

It can only be a matter of time before punk rock, currently the laughing stock or *bête noir* of all serious music critics, has its abrasiveness and effervescence recognized as the symptoms of genius, and its leading practitioners are placed on pedestals beside Bach, Beethoven and the Beatles.

Yet for the moment the unseemly criticism of current popular music continues:

T he effect of rock and roll on young people is to turn them into devil worshippers, to stimulate self-expression through sex, to provoke lawlessness, impair nervous stability and destroy the sanctity of marriage. It is an evil influence on the youth of our country.

Reverend Albert Carter, Pentecostal Minister

R ock and Roll is a means of pulling the White Man down to the level of the Negro. It is part of a plot to undermine the morals of the youth of our nation.

Secretary of the North Alabama White Citizens Council

Nor are members of the popular music fraternity above criticizing their own business.

> Message songs, as everybody knows, are a drag. It's only college newspaper editors and single girls under fourteen that could possibly have time for them.
>
> **Bob Dylan**

Presumably that was during one of the phases when he was *not* singing message songs.

Sometimes, though, it is neither the actual music nor its influence which is being attacked, but something as innocuous as a name.

> They may be world famous, but four shrieking monkeys are not going to use a privileged family name without permission.
>
> **Frau Eva von Zeppelin**

But, of course, the rock group Led Zeppelin *has* used a privileged family name, for some twelve years.

Staying with German commentators, Adolf Hitler could perhaps have been prophesying the rise of punk rock when he said this about the English:

> They love music, but their love is not returned.
>
> 1941

Oddballs

There was no doubt about [Harold] Wilson's godship, said Speller, and that was why *Occult News* was backing him. We were living in a theocracy and the ruling god had to be supported. I asked Speller if Wilson knows he is a god, and Speller thought probably not yet. The knowledge would come gradually.

The Sun, c. 1970

Leaving aside the question of whether (as certain political opponents insisted) Sir Harold Wilson did indeed become convinced of his godhood later in his career, we present a chapter of strange cults and strange doings. It is full of useful facts: did you know that the question of heredity *versus* environment is of concern to werewolves?

As I have already stated, in some people lycanthropy is hereditary; and when it is not hereditary it may be acquired through the performance of certain of the rites ordained by Black Magic.

Elliot O'Donnell, *Werwolves*, 1912

Other cultists felt that magicians probably knew all about science:

We are suggesting that it would not have been impossible for certain intellectually gifted scientists (alchemists) to have mastered radio transmission, powered heavier-than-air flight, and many other discoveries about the time Columbus discovered America.

Brad Steiger & Joan Whritenour, *New UFO Breakthrough*, 1968

In general, the founders and members of what we are so rude as to call 'nut cults' have far more insight into the cosmos than mere scientists *or* alchemists:

86

To know of the earth's concavity is to know God, while to believe in the earth's convexity is to deny Him and all His works.

Cyrus Reed Teed, c. 1890

The idea of a sun millions of miles in diameter and 91,000,000 miles away [*sic*] is silly. The sun is only 32 miles across and not more than 3,000 miles from the earth. It stands to reason it must be so. God made the sun to light the earth, and therefore must have placed it close to the task it was designed to do. What would you think of a man who built a house in Zion [Illinois] and put the lamp to light it in Kenosha, Wisconsin?

Wilbur Glenn Voliva, c. 1915

And the ancient Egyptians, of course, not only knew everything but recorded it for posterity in a clear and simple manner which only benighted Egyptologists cannot understand.

The Great Pyramid is a geometrical representation of the mathematical basis of the science of a former civilization. This former civilization had condensed its knowledge of natural law into a single general formula, and the application of this formula was analogous to the modern application of Einstein's Theory of Relativity. The universal application of this formula in the world of this former civilization left its impress on every form of constructional expression, whether ethical, literary or artistic ... The Egyptian Records define the geometrical dimensions of a Standard Pyramid that constitutes the geometrical expression of the ancient Law of Relativity.

D. Davidson & H. Aldersmith, *The Great Pyramid: Its Divine Message*, 1924

In other words, rather than *write down* their infallible prophecies of the future, the Egyptians mysteriously built them into convenient mnemonic shapes, such as pyramids. Future students will doubtless show that our 'law' of Relativity has influenced architecture and that the Post Office Tower in London is built in the shape of $E = mc^2$.

Einstein, as will be seen elsewhere, was harshly treated by many reputable scientists—surely off-beat cultists would be kinder?

E instein a scientist? It were difficult to imagine anyone more contrary and opposite to what a scientist should be ... As a rational scientist Einstein is a fair violinist. Einstein is already dead and buried, alongside Andersen, Grimm, and the Mad Hatter.

George Francis Gillette, 1929

Gillette's down-to-earth cosmology gave us 'Gravitation is the kicked back nut of the screwing bolt of radiation', 'Gravitation and backscrewing are synonymous', and other gems of cosmic insight.

Far more sensible than Einstein, to some, was Hans Hörbiger and his delightful World Ice Theory: some German comments on this are quoted by Willy Ley:

O ur Nordic ancestors grew strong in ice and snow: belief in the World Ice is consequently the natural heritage of Nordic Man.

J ust as it needed a child of Austrian culture—Hitler!— to put the Jewish politicians in their place, so it needed an Austrian [Hörbiger] to cleanse the world of Jewish science.

T he Führer, by his very life, has proved how much a so-called 'amateur' can be superior to self-styled professionals: it needed another 'amateur' to give us complete understanding of the universe . . . .

Hörbiger, being a mining engineer, was well equipped to argue that, for example, the moon has a coating of ice 140 miles thick. A much more successful amateur (though later he was to award himself numerous degrees and even, for a while, a doctorate) was L. Ron Hubbard, the founder of Scientology, formerly termed Dianetics. As a science-fiction writer he gave his followers a run for their money: Christopher Evans in *Cults of Unreason* quotes a marvellous passage wherein Hubbard describes his scientology-powered trip to heaven at a rather exact time:

43,891,832,611,177 years, 344 days, 10 hours, 20 minutes and 40 seconds from 10.02½ pm, Daylight Greenwich Time, 9 May 1963.

Heaven's gates, Hubbard reports, are

> ... well done, well built. An avenue of statues of saints leads up to them. The gate pillars are supported by marble angels. The entering grounds are very well kept, laid out like the Bush Gardens in Pasadena ...

Obviously the thrones, emerald rainbows, thunder and lightning and the sea of crystal mentioned in *Revelation* had been subject to urban renewal by the late date Hubbard mentions. Dianetics in its original form was a form of psychotherapy (see under Medicine) whose effects were dramatic:

> One sees with some sadness that more than three quarters of the world's population will become subject to the remaining quarter as a natural consequence about which we can do exactly nothing.
>
> **L. Ron Hubbard,** *c.* **1950**

Certainly Scientologists gained curious powers, as shown by their resourcefulness when banned from entering Britain:

> Commenting on the airport check, he said: 'They are going to have a great deal of trouble because they now have information to the effect that scientologists are disguising themselves as people.'
>
> *Daily Telegraph, c.* **1970**

Against such talent, law and order is powerless! And, speaking of law and order, we should quote a couple of very 'oddball' sayings from people having nothing whatever to do with odd cults:

> A witness cannot give evidence of his age unless he can remember being born.
>
> **Judge Blagden, 1950**

> Baader had the perfidy to shoot himself in the back of his head to try to make us look like murderers.
>
> **Werner Maihofer, West German Interior Minister, 1977**

The flying-saucer cults had varied effects:

> I am convinced that UFOs exist, because I have seen one.
> **President James Carter, 1976**

> 40-year-old Mr Searl, father of six, says his group could produce a full-sized saucer which could reach the Moon in two seconds. All they need is £12,000,000 and a bit of official encouragement. **Sunday Mirror, c. 1970**

This time, however, law and order felt itself able to cope:

> The flights, landings and take-offs of airships called 'flying saucers' and 'flying cigars' of any nationality are forbidden on the territory of the community of Châteauneuf-du-Pape.
> **Decree by Mayor of community, 1954**

And a line from the man who was a one-man cult with a strange sense of humour (not inherited by all of his modern followers):

> I think, myself, that it would be absurd to say that the whole sky is gelatinous; it seems more acceptable that only certain areas are. **Charles Fort, New Lands, 1923**

Earlier, in the 1890s, there was widespread interest in Atlantis; not as the formerly volcanic Mediterranean island of Thēra, which blew up around 1500BC and perhaps inspired Plato's Atlantis parable more than a thousand years later, but as a great continent occupying much of the Atlantic Ocean at a very early date:

> The first map represents the land surface of the earth as it existed about a million years ago, when the Atlantean Race was at its height, and before the first great submergence took place about 800,000 years ago.
> **W. Scott-Elliot, The Story of Atlantis, 1896**

This book and similar volumes were produced by the Theosophical Publishing Society, some of whose members were lucky enough to have been the recipients of much fascinating information on Atlantis and other ancient mysteries, transmitted to them by unspecified psychic means:

A s readers of Theosophic literature may know, wheat was not evolved on this planet at all. It was the gift of the Manu who brought it from another globe outside our chain of worlds.

Ibid.

A s readers of the *Transaction of the London Lodge* on the 'Pyramids and Stonehenge' will know, the rude simplicity of Stonehenge was intended as a protest against the extravagant ornament and over-decoration of the existing temples in Atlantis ...

Ibid.

Never mind that Stonehenge was built several thousand years after the last remnants of Atlantis disappeared beneath the waves; perhaps something was lost in translation. Even so, the Atlantean civilization apparently attained great heights:

There were no recognised physicians in those days— every educated man knew more or less of medicine as well as of magnetic healing ... The occult properties of plants, metals and precious stones, as well as the alchemical processes of transmutation, were included in this category.

Ibid.

I f the system of water supply in the 'City of the Golden Gates' was wonderful, the Atlantean methods of locomotion must be recognised as still more marvellous, for the airship or flying-machine ... was then a realised fact. ...When metal was used [in its construction] it was generally an alloy ... white-coloured, like aluminium, and even lighter in weight. Over the rough framework of the air-boat was extended a large sheet of this metal which was then beaten into shape and electrically welded where necessary ...

Ibid.

It does seem a shame that such an advanced civilization, after having endured for almost a million years, should have been totally destroyed, together with every single one of its artefacts, by earthquake and inundation of sea-water in the year 9564BC.

Moving into more dubious territory, we have the hoaxers—and two particularly famous and widely accepted ones deserve mention. Firstly, the telescopic discovery of life on the Moon, which appeared as a succession of exclusive news items in the New York *Sun* during August 1835: it was claimed that the observations were being made by the well-known astronomer Sir John Herschel, at the Cape of Good Hope (too far distant for the story to be quickly verified or denied). Each day's despatch claimed an even greater marvel:

The specimen of lunar vegetation, however, which they had already seen, had decided a question of too exciting an interest to induce them to retard its exit. It had demonstrated that the moon has an atmosphere constituted similarly to our own, and capable of sustaining organized, and therefore, most probably, animal life.

Richard Locke, *The Great Moon Hoax***, 1835**

'The trees,' says Dr Grant, 'for a period of ten minutes, were of one unvaried kind, and unlike any I have seen, except the largest class of yews in the English churchyards, which they in some respects resemble.'

Ibid.

Dr Herschel has classified not less than thirty-eight species of forest trees, and nearly twice this number of plants, found in this tract alone, which are widely different from those found in more equatorial latitudes. Of animals, he classified nine species of mammalia, and five of oviparia. Among the former kind is a small kind of reindeer, the elk, the moose, the horned bear, and the biped beaver.

Ibid.

But whilst gazing upon [the crags] in a perspective of about half a mile, we were thrilled with astonishment to perceive four successive flocks of large winged creatures, wholly unlike any kind of birds, descend with a slow even motion from the cliffs on the western side, and alight upon the plain . . .

This lens, being soon introduced, gave us a fine half-mile distance; and we counted three parties of these creatures, of twelve, nine and fifteen in number, walking erect towards a small wood near the base of the eastern precipices. Certainly they *were* like human beings, for their wings had now disappeared, and their attitude in walking was both erect and dignified ... They averaged four feet in height, were covered, except on the face, with short and glossy copper-colored hair, and had wings composed of a thin membrane, without hair, lying snugly upon their backs, from the top of the shoulders to the calves of the legs ... these creatures were evidently engaged in conversation; their gesticulation, more particularly the varied action of their hands and arms, appeared impassioned and emphatic. We hence inferred that they were rational beings ...

Ibid.

All these reports, even the last, were initially believed, and the *Sun*'s circulation soared accordingly. Details were widely reprinted as news in American and European newspapers.

The Great Moon Hoax was nicely calculated to take in a nineteenth-century public already informed that even the Sun might be inhabited (see our chapter on Astronomy), and happy to accept that other worlds might swarm with familiar livestock, from reindeer to beavers. Characteristically, one of the most successful hoaxes of the twentieth century dealt with the odd ways of the nineteenth: this was the celebrated bathtub of H. L. Mencken. The original (fictitious) story appeared in 1917 and is summarized in Curtis MacDougall's *Hoaxes*, 1958:

The first American bathtub was displayed December 10, 1842, by Adam Thompson of Cincinnati ... constructed of mahogany and lined with lead; he inaugurated it with a stag party at which the entertainment consisted of trying it out ... Physicians denounced the bathtub as a menace to public health. In Boston a city ordinance prohibited its use except upon medical advice. Virginia imposed a thirty dollar tax on each installation of a bathtub. Hartford, Conneticut, Wilmington, Delaware and Providence, Rhode Island, all charged extra rates for water used in bathtubs. The

Philadelphia city council considered an ordinance forbidding its use from November to May, but the measure was defeated by two votes ...

MacDougall goes on to list approximately sixty books and newspaper articles quoting this nonsense as pure fact, from 1917 through to 1954. Doubtless he missed a good many; doubtless more people have been taken in since MacDougall's book appeared, for the numerous exposures of this hoax have had no effect whatever. Mencken himself cites the Boston *Herald*, which satirically reprinted the bathtub story in 1927 with the comment 'The American public will swallow anything'—and three weeks later used the material as a piece of news.

Which sets us wondering which of the items we have gathered may not be hoaxes. Surely that rumoured Pennsylvania (or Indiana, depending on the source of your rumour) law to make pi equal to *four* is a little too good to be true? The best we could trace for certain was the Indiana bill to make pi 3.2—and that was defeated by two votes: see the chapter on Science. It is all very worrying.

Politics

T he politics of the world is too serious a business to be
left any more to foreigners.

Spectator, c. **1970**

Serious or not, politics must be one of the most unreliable fields for
prediction—and one of the most popular. Even more so than self-
checking computers and hunters of the Snark, politicians devoutly
believe 'What I tell you three times is true', and emit their hopes
and desires as truth, again and again until the voters' incredulity is
(in theory) overwhelmed. Election promises cannot perhaps be
counted—thus reducing the potential length of this chapter from
several libraries' worth to manageable size—but many dogmatic
statements still come to mind. We remember Harold Wilson
doggedly repeating that 'the pound in your pocket' would be
unaffected by the 1970s devaluation, even as the resulting inflation
soared. On the other side of the UK political fence, a Conservative-
commissioned poll predicted a massive Conservative victory in the
Heath *vs.* Wilson election, only for Wilson's Labour party to win
after all. The subtle reason for this failure was that the impartial
pollsters had taken a random sample of names from the telephone
directory; the average Labour voter, being poorer than the average
Conservative, was less likely to own a telephone!
Some eminent opinions of British political development:

N ationalism will be the Magna Carta of the twentieth
century.

H. G. Wells, 1920

I know of no method by which an aristocratic nation
like England can become a democracy.

Hilaire Belloc, 1921

Of course, the new political movement causing most fuss in this
century was Communism. It was well over a hundred years ago that
Karl Marx observed that capitalism was dying; when the Russian
revolution finally came, there were outbreaks of wishful thinking on
every side.

95

In my opinion the attempt to build up a Communist republic on the lines of strongly centralised State Communism, under the iron rule of the dictatorship of a party, is ending in failure.

Prince Kropotkin, 1920

England is at last ripe for revolution.

Leon Trotsky, 1925

The inference to which I am led by my study is that England is heading rapidly toward an era of great revolutionary upheavals.

Leon Trotsky, 1925

And the revolution could do nothing but good; despite the carpings of the vile decadent West, Russia was revealed as being a rather jolly place:

Gaiety is the most outstanding feature of the Soviet Union.

Joseph Stalin, 1935

More good news was on the way:

It will take some time for the lesson of Spain to be learned, but increasingly it will be recognised that the Communist Party has ceased to be revolutionary.

Fenner Brockway, 1937

Obviously Communism would be no more problem; but in its early days, Socialism was feared to much the same extent, and pronounced dead on all possible occasions.

We have reached a point where we can look back and see that the Socialist movement in Western Europe has failed.

John Middleton Murry, 1933

I t is certain as the day that a Labour town council, a Socialist or Communist government, would not for a day tolerate strikes in social or other services necessary for the life of the nation.

George Lansbury, 1934

Although it has developed an increased tolerance for strikes, Socialism is still plugging away and moving steadily towards the millennium:

W e thought we could put the economy right in five years. We were wrong. It will probably take ten.

Anthony Wedgwood Benn, 1968

Mention of the economy inevitably reminds us of Keynes and his interesting joint solution to the problems of unemployment and benefit:

I f the Treasury were to fill old bottles with banknotes, bury them at suitable depths in disused coalmines which are then filled up to the surface with town rubble, and leave it to private enterprise on well-tried principles of *laissez-faire* to dig the notes up again ... there need be no more unemployment and, with the help of the repercussions, the real income of the community ... would probably become a good deal larger than it actually is.

John Maynard Keynes, *The General Theory of Employment, Interest and Money*, **1936**

Not to be confused with Socialism was Hitler's 'National Socialism', about which much was said before and during the Second World War:

W e are winning international respect.

Adolf Hitler, 1934

I t [the Sudetenland] is the last territorial claim that I have to make in Europe.

Adolf Hitler, 1938

I believe it is peace for our time . . . peace with honour.

Neville Chamberlain, radio speech, 1st October 1938

A ny alliance whose purpose is not the intention to wage war is senseless and useless.

Adolf Hitler

H itler has missed the bus.

Neville Chamberlain, speech in anticipation of German landing in Norway

I think Hitler was too moderate.

J. B. Stoner

A jolly footnote to World War II is given in Professor Arthur Butz's book *The Hoax of the Twentieth Century*: referring to the attempted extermination of Jews, Professor Butz says:

A n historic lie . . . the most tragic imposture of all time.

And he goes on to show how many less-than-liberal remarks (see our chapter on Race) were thrust into the mouths of upstanding SS men by the filthy propagandists of America.

The 'thirties also saw the rise of Fascism, generally distinguishable from Nazism by its name and the fact that it occurred in different places. (The theory that it made the trains run on time has now been demolished.)

F ascism is a religion; the twentieth century will be known in history as the century of Fascism.

Benito Mussolini, on the occasion of Hitler's seizure of power

In England, too, the Fascist party was filled with optimism:

W e shall reach the helm within five years.

Sir Oswald Mosley, 1938

B efore the organization of the Blackshirt movement free speech did not exist in this country.

Sir Oswald Mosley

One common misconception about Fascism was that it was an extreme right-wing movement:

> I am not, and never have been, a man of the right. My position was on the left and is now in the centre of politics.
>
> **Sir Oswald Mosley, *The Times*, letter, 1968**

Right-wing activities in America included the 'reign of terror' of Senator Joseph McCarthy, of 'Are you now or have you ever been a Communist?' fame; indeed, the whole McCarthy anti-communist craze resembled nothing so much as a Soviet purge. But some people thought it was a great idea:

> Someday the American people will erect a monument to his [McCarthy's] memory.
>
> **Eddie Rickenbacker**

> You hear about 'constitutional rights', 'free speech' and the 'free press'. Every time I hear these words I say to myself, 'That man is a Red!' . . . You never hear a *real* American talk like that!
>
> **Mayor Frank Hague**

> What are our schools for if not indoctrination against Communism?
>
> **Richard M. Nixon**

> *Communism Is 20th Century Americanism.*
>
> **Pamphlet put out by the Communist Party USA, 1936**

How did that last one get in there? Anyway, much more excitement was due in the 1970s, with Watergate:

> Writing about the Nixon Administration is about as exciting as covering the Prudential Life Assurance Company.
>
> **Art Buchwald, July 1970**

I reject the cynical view that politics is inevitably, or even usually, dirty business.

President Richard Nixon, August 1973

There can be no whitewash at the White House.

President Richard Nixon, December 1973

Watergate is just an attack by the niggers and the Jews and the commies on Nixon.

Attributed to Mike Curb, then President of MGM Records

In fact there does seem to be a backlash of pro-Nixon feeling after the whole dreadful mess of Watergate, and had we waited a few years more we could surely have quoted extensively from books depicting the former President as a cruelly martyred saint, an innocent thrown to the wolves by the monstrous anti-democratic forces of the CIA.

Following Nixon, President Gerald Ford brought a refreshing brand of originality to White House statements. We feel that suggestions of his having played too much football without a helmet during his younger days are merely unfortunate exaggerations by those unable to appreciate the subtlety of his wit. For example, in December 1975 he proposed a toast to Anwar Sadat, 'the President of Israel', and the following year he declared: 'There is no Soviet domination of Eastern Europe'. Let us move, with an immense effort, to Africa.

We are all satisfied in South Africa now.

General Smuts, 1926

In view of the success of my economic revolution in Uganda, I offer myself to be appointed Head of the Commonwealth.

Idi Amin, 1975

Rhodesia/Zimbabwe has lately been more in the news than other parts of Africa; of course it was all the fault of Cecil Rhodes in the first place:

I admire him [Rhodes], I frankly confess it; and when his time comes I shall buy a piece of the rope for a keepsake.

Mark Twain, *Following the Equator***, 1897**

Opinions on the future of colonies in general have never been lacking:

The cession of any Colony or Protectorate—save as the result of a crushing defeat in war—is simply unthinkable and would never be accepted by the nation.

Lord Lugard, 1938

And the subject of Rhodesia drew some more specific comments:

Mr John Stokes (C., Oldbury and Halesowen) asked why white Rhodesians should give up everything just for some half-baked untried theory of one man, one vote.

Financial Times, c. **1970**

We now have a Rhodesian constitution and if anybody thinks it can be improved, I would like to know where.

Ian Smith, 1971

We have the happiest Africans in the world.

Ian Smith, 1971

There are going to be no dramatic changes in Rhodesia.

Ian Smith, 1975

I don't believe in black majority rule ever in Rhodesia, not in a thousand years.

Ian Smith, 1976

The cumulative effects of the economic and financial
sanctions [against Rhodesia] might well bring the
rebellion to an end within a matter of weeks rather than
months.

Harold Wilson, January 1966

Perhaps all these evident difficulties in political prediction could be
resolved by the aid of science. A noted astronomer, Dr Ernst J.
Opik, has carefully correlated sunspot activity with revolutionary
political activity in his book *The Oscillating Universe*. The link
between the two, he says, 'cannot possibly be due to coincidence'.
This and similar relationships deserve further investigation; we
ourselves have noticed how otherwise sane folk can turn into
political spokesmen when the moon is full.

Race

Why would we have different races if God meant us to be alike and associate with one another?

Lester Maddox

The little matter of race has produced some of the most disagreeably and determinedly *wrong* utterances in all history. As a rough generalization, coloured people and Jews have suffered most—the former for their intolerable habit of looking different from your average white person, the latter for their even more insidious practice of looking the same. The most definite opinions on Jewishness were of course expressed by a certain German regime.

The non-Nordic man takes up an intermediate position between the Nordic man and the . . . ape.

Herman Gauch, *New Elements of Scientific Investigation*, 1934

The blood particles of a Jew are completely different from those of a Nordic man. Hitherto one [a Jew] has prevented this fact being proved by microscopic investigation.

Julius Streicher, 1935

Christ cannot possibly have been a Jew. I don't have to prove that scientifically. It is a fact!

Joseph Paul Goebbels

Thank God, I've always avoided persecuting my enemies.

Adolf Hitler, 1941

Others, of course, had their comments to add:

Science shows us the infinite superiority of the Teutonic Aryan over all others, and it therefore becomes us to see that his ascendancy shall remain undisputed. Any racial mixture can but lower the result. The Teutonic race, whether in Scandinavia, other parts of the continent, England, or America, is the cream of humanity . . .

H. P. Lovecraft, US horror writer, 1916

A n American is either a Jew, or an anti-Semite, unless he is both at the same time.

Jean-Paul Sartre, *Altona*

T here is no anti-Semitism in Russia. In fact, many of my best friends are Jews.

Alexei Kosygin, 1971

Russian anti-Semitism (however nonexistent) seems to have had its effect on Russian writers like Gorky. James Agate reports the following conversation with Edgar Lustgarten:

E.L.: 'James, do you know the passage in Gorky in which he quotes the letter of Pliny to the Emperor Trajan? . . . "It soon transpired that there were many Jews—this is usually the case when one begins to investigate a crime."'
J.A.: 'What's remarkable about that?'
E.L.: 'Only that Pliny wrote "Christians", not "Jews".'

James Agate, *Ego 6*, 1944

Hitler had his own views on the Russians, incidentally.

B y instinct, the Russian does not incline towards a higher form of society.

1941

More dismissive comments on black people came to light than on almost anything else we researched (except, possibly, women). Even well-intentioned men have uttered odd comments, and the first of those who follow may come as a surprise:

T here is a physical difference between the White and Black races which I believe will forever forbid the two races living together on terms of social and political equality.   **Abraham Lincoln, speech, 1858**

Whether they will ever produce a man of genius is an idle and unimportant question; they can at least gain their livelihood as labourers and artisans. They are therefore of service to their country; let them have fair play, and they will find their right place whatever it may be. As regards the social question, they will no doubt, like the Jews, intermarry always with their own race, and will thus remain apart.

Winwood Reade, *The Martyrdom of Man,* **1872**

I deplore the fact that throughout the South today subversive elements are attempting to convince the Negro that he should be placed on social equality with white people.

Martin Dies

Or, to reduce the point to its simplest terms:

I ain't going to let no darkies and white folks segregate together in this town.

Eugene Connor, Police Commissioner of Birmingham, Alabama, 1950

By the undemanding process of not educating people, it was possible to dismiss them as uneducated—or even impossible to educate. Again, not much comment is needed:

The grown-up Negro partakes, as regards his intellectual facilities, of the nature of the child, the female, and the senile White.

Carl Vogt, natural history professor, 1860s

In the skull of the negro the cranial capacity and the brain itself is much undersized. On the average [the Negro skull] will hold thirty-five fluid ounces, as against forty-five for the Caucasian skull. In the negro the cranial bones are dense and unusually thick, converting the head into a veritable battering-ram. Moreover, the cranial sutures unite firmly very early in life. This checks the development of the brain long before that takes place in other races, and this fact accounts to some extent for the more or less sudden stunting of the Ethiopian intellect shortly after arriving at puberty.

Robert W. Shufeldt, *The Negro a Menace to American Civilisation*, 1907

Alarmingly, the encyclopaedias began to get in on the act:

Generally speaking, the negro is greatly inferior mentally to the white and yellow races, and this has been attributed by some to the early closing of the cranial sutures, by which the normal development of the brain is arrested.

The Waverley Encyclopaedia, c. 1930

They occupy rather a low level in the scale of humanity, and are lacking in those mental and moral qualities which have impressed the stamp of greatness on other races that have distinguished themselves in the history of the world.

The Nuttall Encyclopaedia, 1930

Percolating ever downwards, this theory eventually reached the duller species of politician, whose sutures had clearly been riveted at birth:

Evidently you did not try to learn anything until you had reached maturity, because you know it is a biological fact that a Negro's skull, where the parts of it are connected by sutures, ossifies by the time a Negro reaches maturity and they become unable to take in information.

US Senator Bilbo, 1945, letter to a black teacher in a Chicago school, whom he advised to work as a charwoman

At rock-bottom level:

We are not just a bunch of illiterate Southern nigger-killers. We are good, white, Christian people, hard-working people working for a White America.

When one of your wives or one of your sisters gets raped by a nigger, maybe you'll get smart and join the Klan.

Mary Bacon, US jockey, speaking at a Ku Klux Klan meeting in Louisiana

Unfortunately this form of moronic nonsense is not yet dead. In his excellent book *The Other Glass Teat*, Harlan Ellison quotes passages from a racist US newspaper of hopefully small circulation. The following letter from a 'Miss K.S.' appeared under the headline '15 YEAR OLD PASADENA GIRL TELLS OF SCHOOL TERROR':

I would never go into a swimming pool where there has been or are Niggers in it. I refused to take swimming for that reason. My mother phoned the Board of Education and stated as much. They could not understand such a thing as they said no one had ever refused to take swimming for that purpose. My mother told me she was proud that I was the first to refuse, but she prayed I wouldn't be the last ... The next day I was told by the head physical education teacher that '*the Niggers are the same as whites, and the skin was the only difference!*' I told her maybe they were as good as her, but they sure were not as good as I am!

The Thunderbolt, **November 1970**

Meanwhile, in unprejudiced Britain, the *New Statesman* culled the following tasty items (1968–1974):

One employer gave as his reason for not employing a coloured school-leaver: 'Your pigmentation would make you more allergic to frostbite in our frozen food.'

Daily Telegraph

Most of the boarding-houses here are not large enough to take coloured and white guests at the same time.

Mrs Dorothy Brookes of the Withernsea, Yorkshire, Land-ladies Association

Oh yes, we Tory councillors have done a lot for race relations. I do think it's very important. After all, but for the Grace of God, we'd be black ourselves, wouldn't we?

Conservative woman councillor

Readers responding to the above with a healthy surge of nausea should know that they are not alone.

Religion

In the beginning . . .

The like structure of humans of all races and the fact that they can all intermarry and produce children point to our having descended from an original human pair, male and female. Why, then, should we balk at calling these ancestors Adam and Eve?

Is the Bible Really the Word of God?, Watchtower
Bible & Tract Society, 1969, first edition of 9,000,000 copies

So what does the evidence show? That there is every reason to accept the Genesis account of creation as a fact. While it is at odds with certain *theories*, it harmonizes with proved scientific *fact*. It reaches out far beyond details of limited value and provides answers to questions of life that are of greatest concern to all of us.

Ibid.

This particular writer goes on to explain how Noah was able to get, for example, every member of the cat family into the Ark—he simply took along a pair of domestic cats and bred them up into lions, tigers, panthers, leopards and so forth once he had landed.

Many a strange thing has been said in the name of religion, and as a result this chapter leaps about more than most. The problem of resurrection, for example.

The thirteenth-century book, *La Lumière as Lais*, claimed that at the Last Judgement the blessed would arise with all senses functioning, and all at the physical age of thirty-two years and three months. A twelfth-century mosaic in Torcello Cathedral shows those who had been eaten and digested by animals being regurgitated intact. (Dare we ask you to contemplate the accomplishment of this feat by a rat?)

In 1273, the Bishop of Tusculum stated that, when Satan and his companions were originally driven out of Heaven, their numbers came to 133,306,668, leaving behind 266,613,336 unfallen angels. As there is supposed to be a Guardian Angel for each individual on

Earth, this creates certain numerical problems: but an English heraldic writer, Randle Holme, made it all quite clear in 1688 when he wrote that 'there remained still in Heaven . . . more Angels than there was, is, and shall be'.

Debates on the number of angels and whether, say, two angels could occupy the same space (something which really was discussed—while the famous problem of 'how many angels could dance on the point of a pin?' was made up as a satire on such theology) were relatively innocuous. This could not last.

> Thou shalt not suffer a witch to live.   **Exodus xxii, 18**

This text was used enthusiastically, and many subtly conceived tests of witchcraft brought into play. Ordeal By Water was a famous one: they tied you up and tossed you in; if you failed to drown you were a witch and would be burnt. Another process was to weigh a person suspected of witchery against a Bible. If the Bible seemed heavier, the accused was acquitted. The inventor of Wesleyan Methodism defended the theory of witches:

> The giving up of witchcraft is in effect the giving up of the Bible.   **John Wesley**

After quoting this, Bertrand Russell nastily added, 'I think he was right.'

If the hand of Man did not smite evil-doers, the hand of God would surely have a go . . . The 1755 Massachusetts earthquakes were caused by lightning conductors ('the iron points invented by the sagacious Mr Franklin'), since to avoid lightning was to defy God's justice. As the Reverend Dr Price put it in 1755:

> In Boston are more erected than elsewhere in New England, and Boston seems to be more dreadfully shaken. Oh! there is no getting out of the mighty hand of God.

Then, again:

> When in 1894 the spire of St Mary's fell in Shrewsbury, severely damaging the church, the Reverend Mr Poyntz, the rector, preached a special sermon, saying that it was thrown down because the people were organising a memorial to Darwin, a Shrewsbury man.

> **Bergen Evans, *The Natural History of Nonsense***

But of course God had special rules for women:

The ministrations of a male priesthood do not normally arouse that side of female human nature which should be quiescent during the times of the adoration of almighty God [whereas] it would be impossible for the male members of the average Anglican congregation to be present at a service at which a woman ministered without becoming unduly conscious of her sex.

Commission appointed by Archbishop of Canterbury, c.1935

That last was quoted by Bergen Evans (*ibid.*), who adds: 'Of course Quakers have had female ministers for centuries and their meetings are not particularly distinguished for libidinousness, but this may only mean that Quakers are less virile than Anglicans.'

One eminently orthodox Catholic divine laid it down that a confessor may fondle a nun's breasts, provided he does it without evil intent.

Bertrand Russell, *Unpopular Essays*, 1950

The question of morality, viewed through religious eyes, was always a complicated one. Probably not many modern readers will realize just how unspeakable and decadent it is to wear gloves, or socks:

Musonius, a philosopher, who lived at the close of the first century of Christianity, among other invectives against the corruption of the age, says, 'It is shameful that persons in perfect health should clothe their hands and feet with soft and hairy coverings.'

Isaac Disraeli, *Curiosities of Literature*, 1791–3

Morality aside, we know that God's planning makes contraception unnecessary:

Our Heavenly Father never sends us more mouths than He can feed.

Henry M. Guernsey, *Plain Talks on Avoided Subjects*, 1882

His views on racial questions have been made known to a chosen few:

I t is my conviction that God ordained segregation.

Reverend Billy James Hargis, presumably not so long ago

Above all, He exists:

A nd now the announcement of Watson and Crick about DNA. This is for me the real proof of the existence of God.

Salvador Dali, in an especially silly mood

One wonders whether Dali knew of US Patent 1,087,186 (1914), for a device, consisting of two intertwined helices or springs, which was supposed to demonstrate the existence of God. And speaking of science, it seems that choosing the right religion can help a lot:

T he man of scientific discoveries *is something more mentally* than the man of science who calls himself a scientist without *contributing one pennyworth to science*. Usually these men are *free-thinking* scientists. The Papal Academy of Science had their birth of Science in early times, obtained mastery over many mysteries of nature ... The Jesuit astronomers are the greatest of the first rank of scientists, and some are the world's master mathematicians. The world's thinkers credit the Papal scientists as far in advance of all others in the scientific field of enquiry.

Timothy O'Mahoney Esq, *Philosophy of God's Mathematics of the Atomic Energy*, 1948

These freethinkers and unbelievers get everywhere these days, and cause the most annoying problems:

C hristianity will go. It will vanish and shrink. I needn't argue about that. I'm right and will be proved right. We're more popular than Jesus now.

John Lennon of the Beatles, 1966

S ometimes I have a devil of a job convincing ghosts they are actually dead.

Canon John Pearce-Higgins, on exorcism, 1973

It might be complained that this most devotional of chapters has concentrated unfairly on Christianity. We do have one Islamic snippet from the recent news:

A t another airbase, mullahs actually instructed aircrews to bomb the American reconnaissance satellite when it appeared over Iran.

***The Times*, 11 July 1980**

Faith may still move mountains, but it seems it cannot attain orbital velocity.

Science

You know, Tolstoy, like myself, wasn't taken in by superstitions like science and medicine.

George Bernard Shaw

Several other notables have sternly resisted being taken in by this absurd superstition of science:

I am tired of all this sort of thing called science here ... We have spent millions in that sort of thing for the last few years, and it is time it should be stopped.

Senator Simon Cameron, on the Smithsonian Institute, 1901

The only thing that science has done for men in the last hundred years is to create for him fresh moral problems.

Most Reverend Geoffrey Fisher, Archbishop of Canterbury, 1950

Modern physics is an instrument of Jewry for the destruction of Nordic science ... True physics is the creation of the German spirit.

Rudolf Tomaschek, 1930s

Einstein and people like Einstein said that the world was flat. Einstein and people like Einstein said Man would never travel faster than the speed of sound.

T. Lobsang Rampa, *Chapters of Life*, 1967

We wonder what all these people thought scientists actually did— apart from spending money, inventing troublesome moral problems, destroying the Nordic spirit and insisting the world was flat. One clue is given by Hilaire Belloc's demolition of the silly idea that any form of ability was required:

Anyone of common mental and physical health can practise scientific research ... Anyone can try by patient experiment what happens if this or that substance be mixed in this or that proportion with some other under this or that condition. Anyone can vary the experiment in any number of ways. He that hits in this fashion on something novel and of use will have fame ... The fame will be the product of luck and industry. It will not be the product of special talent.

Hilaire Belloc, *Essays of a Catholic Layman in England,* **1931**

Likewise, anyone can write great books. Simply vary the mixture of words in any number of ways. Anyone can paint great paintings ... What was that about an infinite number of monkeys?

Science, we know, is hard to understand:

For sphaerical bodies move by fives, and every globular figure placed upon a plane, in direct volutation, returns to the first point of contaction in the fifth touch, accounting by the Axes of the Diameters or Cardinall points of the four quarters thereof. And before it arriveth unto the same point again, it maketh five circles equall unto itself, in each progress from those quarters absolving an equall circle.

Sir Thomas Browne, *The Garden of Cyrus*

Science, as Charles Fort used to tell us, is mainly concerned with denying and explaining away the truth:

Ullisses Androvandi, an eminent seventeenth-century zoologist, thought they [flint artefacts] were due to 'An admixture of a certain exhalation of thunder and lightning with metallic matter, chiefly in dark clouds, which is distilled from the circumfused moisture and coagulated into a mass and subsequently indurated by heat, like a brick.'

Ronald Millar, *The Piltdown Men*

And science, as every reader of pulp science fiction was aware, deals mainly with mysterious and potent Rays. This goes all the way back to Ptolemy, who in the second century AD said that it would be impossible for Man to cross the equator, since the directly vertical rays of the Sun would cause the ocean to boil and set fire to wooden ships. It took twelve centuries for Europeans to prove him wrong (though the Arabs in the Indian Ocean were insufficiently advanced, either intellectually or scientifically, to appreciate the inevitability of this danger, and thus succeeded in disproving it at a much earlier date, possibly in the tenth century).

Other comments on Rays follow:

X-rays will prove to be a hoax.

Lord Kelvin, President of the Royal Society, 1890–5

Perhaps Kelvin did well to be cautious—in 1903 the French physicist Prosper Blondlot discovered some wholly fictitious 'N-rays' whose odd properties included that of being refracted by prisms made of aluminium. Only Blondlot, who seems to have suffered from visual hallucinations, could actually detect the rays; when the physicist R. W. Wood stealthily removed the prism, it made no difference to what poor Blondlot thought he saw. On cosmic rays:

Their speed is incredible, approximately that at which light travels, 186,000 miles per second. This is twice as fast as the speed of a bullet leaving the muzzle of a United States Army rifle.

Frank Ross Jr, *Space Ships and Space Travel*, 1956

Just think—all those bullets which missed their targets in World War II were whistling past the Moon a few seconds later, and by now must be close on twenty light-years away!

Red light is actually green. You can prove this by plugging in an electric fire. You get the green light first, and then the red, which are of course inter-changeable. Green is the only true colour, and includes all the other so-called colours of light.

John Bradbury, 'independent cosmologist'

Light is darkness, lit up.

Ibid.

In the early 1960s there was much talk of lasers: it was said that lasers were the death-rays of science fiction, and . . .

... that the problem of destroying missiles in flight could be solved using an intense laser beam ... All such speculations can, however, be dismissed as pure nonsense when a rigorous scientific analysis is applied to the problem.

Professor Hans Thirring, 1963

A laser successfully destroyed an antitank missile in flight at 1km range in 1978.

As shown by the above, science keeps intruding on fields such as warfare and politics. Politics has likewise intruded on science: Lysenkoism (see introduction and our chapter on evolution) is the major example, but it seems that Marxist philosophy also frowns on plate tectonics and the theory of continental drift:

M any hypotheses of geotectonics have caused considerable damage to geotectonics, giving non-specialists the impression that this is a field in which the most superficially conceived fantasy reigns. The clearest example is Wegener's hypothesis of continental drift ... fantastic and nothing to do with science ...

Vladimir Vladimirovich Beloussov, leading Soviet geophysicist, 1954

S omething will certainly remain after the theory of plate tectonics goes. Let us keep our minds open and look for alternatives. I am sure that in the near future we shall need them.

Beloussov, 1979

Fred Hoyle, best known for his more-or-less discredited steady-state theory of the Universe, showed that the existence of continental drift was incompatible with the laws of physics:

H ow then could this [fossil tropical plants found in Greenland] have happened? Not I think through the continents floating around on the surface of the Earth, being sometimes in one place and sometimes in another. How a continent composed of rock some 35 kilometres thick could contrive to move is something that has never been explained, and until some plausible reason is offered in its support we need scarcely take the notion of 'drifting continents' at all seriously.

Frontiers of Astronomy, 1955

But the practical aspects of geology and specifically earthquakes were not properly understood until 1970:

The only way to stop earthquakes is to stop the pressure building up in the first place, and this can only be done by keeping the earth at a constant speed.

P. Norcott, *Bigger and Better Earthquakes*, 1970

In its purest form, science is largely mathematics, and mathematics is less subject than, for instance, biology or geology to the influence of political thought. However, attempts have been made to alter the universal constant pi (π) in conformity with the Bible, which says pi = 3, or with other authorities who found it hard to remember the more exact value 3.141 592 653 589 793 238 462 643 383 279 ... (and so on to infinity). The Indiana state legislature came within a couple of votes of declaring, in 1897, that pi should be made officially equal to 3.2; it is *said* that in the same year that state's General Assembly agreed that pi = 4. In *The New Apocrypha* John Sladek notes other 'exact' fractional values for a number which—it has been proved— cannot be expressed as a simple fraction: 3 9/64, 3 1/7, 3 1/21, 3 1/8, 2 7/9 ... In 1873 the mathematician Shanks calculated pi to 707 decimal places and asked that this value be inscribed on his tombstone: it was, but his last couple of hundred digits were wrong. (Much the same happened to the seventeenth-century mathematician Bernoulli, who was fascinated by the logarithmic spiral curve and wanted one on *his* tomb. The stonecutter carved the wrong sort of spiral.)

Still speaking mathematically:

An American mathematician noticed that the earlier pages in books of logarithms kept in his university library were dirtier than later ones, indicating that science students, for some reason, had more occasion to calculate with numbers beginning with 1 than with any other number. He made a collection of tables and calculated the relative frequency of each digit from 1 to 9. Theoretically they should occur equally often, but he found that 30 per cent of the numbers were 1, whereas 9 only occupied 5 per cent of the space. These are almost exactly the proportions given to these numbers on the scale of a slide rule, so the designers of that instrument clearly recognized that such a bias existed.

Lyall Watson, *Supernature*, 1973

The essential silliness of this lies in the comment about slide-rules. The numbers we actually use are not really random in this way (an example of the sort of thing involved: of the numbers 1–200, about 56 % start with 1 ...). First digits follow a logarithmic pattern; slide-rules are a mechanized way of doing logarithmic calculations, and follow that spacing; Lyall Watson's suggestion that slide-rule manufacturers were trying to give more space to more frequently used numbers is utter nonsense. Let us move (still snarling and spitting) to the still more abstruse mathematical physics of Einstein:

I am still seeking in fact for anything that Einstein has added to mathematical knowledge.

Arthur Lynch, *The Case Against Einstein*, 1932

It has been said that Lynch's anti-Einstein book was the most intelligent of its kind: try, as you read the following, to imagine what the others must have been like.

Einstein and his disciples have merely made a Jezebel of all the worst theories of the mathematicians in the interpretation of the discoveries of Electricity and Optics ... The affair has been cleverly prepared. Memoirs have crowded the German scientific periodicals, full of contradiction and rectifications; then they have announced some sensational results; the contraction of Lorentz, the space of four dimensions of Minkowski; and the popular books have followed before one could criticize these affirmations. [The new science is called Relativity] ... doubtless because it can be understood only by people who have a peculiar conformation of brain, a relativist conformation ... It is of small importance to the relativist to solve the problems if only he has the air of doing so ... His procedure is simple; he takes the results demonstrated by other methods, and he accepts them *a priori*;

afterwards he alters them for his purpose. One searches in vain for an exposition of what he accepts and what he rejects.

A. Duport, Emeritus Professor, Faculty of Science, University of Dijon, approvingly quoted by Lynch, *ibid*.

The principle of special relativity, in the sense of Einstein, constitutes sometimes a redundancy, sometimes an absurdity, according to the domain of its application.

J. Le Roux, quoted by Lynch, *ibid*.

Le Roux's 'investigations of certain doctrines of Relativity have served to disintegrate the whole structure', Lynch added.

But surely Einstein's theories were proved by observation? Not at all:

The Relativists offer three great verifications of their theory, and they claim that on this basis the whole system is justified. These verifications are, as I shall show, nonexistent.

Lynch, *ibid*.

In summary: the shifts of spectral lines produced by the sun's gravity mean nothing because the sun is a long way away. The bending of light as it passes the sun means nothing because not all measurements of the amount of bending agreed exactly. The shifting of the orbit of Mercury means nothing because Einstein fiddled his original equations so as to account for it. Therefore:

I have no doubt that there will arise a new generation who will look with a wonder and amazement, deeper than now accompany Einstein, at our galaxy of thinkers, men of science, popular critics, authoritative professors and witty dramatists, who have been satisfied to waive their common sense in favour of Einstein's absurdities. Then to those will succeed another generation, whose interest will be that of a detached and half-amused contemplation, and in the limbo of forgotten philosophies they may search for the cenotaph of Relativity.

Lynch, *ibid*.

And, sure enough, thirty-seven years later:

E instein's theory is unnecessary.

Harold Aspden, *Physics Without Einstein*, 1969

To be fair, one or two famous names had originally been heard on the anti-Einstein bandwaggon:

I can accept the theory of relativity as little as I can accept the existence of atoms and other such dogma.

Ernst Mach (1838–1916) of Mach number fame

This cleverly brings us to matters atomic, which are largely dealt with in the chapters on energy and warfare. However, there is this:

For example, if every two inches of the circumference of the matter of the world possessed $1\frac{2}{3}$ drams of Radium, the total amount would be 2,737,152,000 drams; this would give us 8,811,456,000 scruples of Radium to every two inches of earth's energy. The radiant energy stored within the atom must ever mean motion, which would lift masses of matter to a height of 280,000 miles ... Now, the atom-producing energy is ever increasing power at a speed of 210,000,000 times faster than velocity [*sic*] of light per second.

Timothy O'Mahoney Esq, *Philosophy of God's Mathematics of the Atomic Energy*, 1948

Sex

W hen a man says he has had pleasure with a woman, he does not mean conversation.

Samuel Johnson

Let us not dwell on the above quotation (Dr Johnson may have been referring only to the pleasures of playing shove ha'penny) ... instead let us talk about sex. This must be one of the all-time favourite conversational topics, far more so than shove ha'penny. Certainly it is a topic on which everybody feels he or she ought to be knowledgeable: many of us have the inclination, most have the requisite apparatus, and nearly all must have read something about it in a book. Doubtless this was how in ancient times Hippocrates learnt that sperm originated in the brain, passing to the testicles *via* the spinal column and thence through the kidneys. The Victorians, though, knew how to deal with books:

C are should be taken not to place books by authors of different sexes next to each other.

Manual of etiquette, 1840s

Undoubtedly the laxness and licentiousness of modern times have led to the enormous increase in the numbers of paperbacks (rather less common in the 1840s). Despite such delicacy as shown by the above, the Victorians had a goodly number of books about s*x, notably Orson Squire Fowler's *Sexual Science* (1870), selections from which have been rescued by William M. Dwyer in his *What Everyone Knew About Sex* (1972):

N eglect or crossness deadens a wife's love, and thereby *shrivels her mammaries*.

T wins and triplets undoubtedly originate in second and third copulations, immediately following the first, each drawing and then impregnating an egg. The fact that twins are born as soon as possible after each other supports this view.

Fowler cites some fascinating theories of how to determine your child's sex. One theory is that the first parent to reach orgasm will thereby cause the child to have the opposite sex (the logic of this is not wholly clear). Or possibly the parent with more 'vital force' will determine the child's sex. Or there was always the German Dr Sixt's wondrous Theory of Testicles:

> He believes that in coition the sperm is injected from one testicle only, the right one producing a boy, the left a girl. If a boy is to be generated, Sixt says, the husband must lie to the right of his wife and put the right knee over first, thus producing tension, which draws up the right testicle into place. 'If,' Sixt states, 'the left testicle should somehow become drawn up towards the abdomen, it may be pushed down quite easily, during coition, and the right one pushed up to be sure of attaining the desired end.'
>
> *Ibid.*

A husband who wished to be utterly safe in going for a boy would perform these interesting exercises just before his lady's period, taking care that he was properly topped up with vital force, that the moon was in its correct phase and that the bed was correctly aligned with the compass, meanwhile being extraordinarily careful to avoid orgasm—which, with all that on his mind, couldn't have been very difficult. Then, with luck, would come pregnancy, a still more hazardous state.

> Do a pregnant mother's experiences affect the offspring? Indeed they do. The eminent Dr Napheys reports the case of a pregnant lady who saw some grapes, longed intensely for them, and constantly thought of them. During her period of gestation she was attacked and much alarmed by a turkey-cock. In due time she gave birth to a child having a large cluster of globular tumours growing from the tongue and exactly resembling our common grapes. And on the child's chest there grew a red excresence exactly resembling a turkey's wattles.
>
> *Ibid.*

Is intercourse during pregnancy really dangerous? Yes, and particularly for the offspring. Mark these facts: If a pregnant woman willingly indulges even though loathing the act, she impresses sexual loathing and disgust on the child. This completely spoils daughters as wives.

Ibid.

We would not want you to think that Fowler had a monopoly in the giving of such helpful advice in all matters sexual, or indeed that he was the first writer on the subject. More than two thousand years earlier Aristotle told people All They Needed to Know about such vital subjects as virility, predetermining the sex of one's children, and pregnancy:

Erection is chiefly caused by scuraum, eringoes, cresses, crysmon, parsnips, artichokes, turnips, asparagus, candied ginger, acorns bruised to powder and drank in muscadel, scallion, sea shell fish, etc.

Aristotle, *The Masterpiece*, fourth century BC

Gentlemen not stuffed with these delicacies who nevertheless find themselves prone to erections should doubtless consult their family doctor or philosopher.

And, if in act of copulation, the woman earnestly look on the man, and fix her mind on him, the child will resemble its father. Nay, if a woman, even in unlawful copulation, fix her mind upon her husband, the child will resemble him though he did not beget it.

Ibid.

The act of coition being over, let the woman repose herself on her right side, with her head lying low, and her body declining, that by sleeping in that posture, the cani, on the right side of the matrix, may prove the place of conception; for therein is the greatest generative heat, which is the chief procuring cause of male children, and rarely fails the expectations of those that experience it . . .

Ibid.

I f it is a male [child conceived], the right breast swells first, the right eye is brighter than the left, the face is high-coloured, because the colour is such as the blood is, and as the male is conceived of purer blood and of more perfect seed than the female.

Ibid.

G alen is of opinion that there is no certain time set for the bearing of children; and that from Pliny's authority, who makes mention of a woman that went thirteen months with child.

Ibid.

If, like us, you have a sneaking suspicion that Galen and Pliny lived somewhat (like three or four hundred years) after Aristotle, all we can say is that our text of *The Masterpiece* dates from the mid-nineteenth century and seems to have been altered a little (in the cause of scientific accuracy, naturally) since Aristotle penned it.

Anyway, let us return to Fowler and listen to him frowning on unnatural sexual acts, such as masturbation:

I f practised in girlhood, does it affect married life? Yes, those girls who practise it fail to develop as women. They become flat-chested and lose the female glow which draws gentlemen around them. They develop amatory vertigo and become very nervous.

Fowler, *ibid.*

A suggested cure for 'self-polluting' women involved the excision of their ovaries. The corresponding cure for men was not, however, recommended—for men in particular the practice carried its own punishment.

A ny other physical signs? Many. Victims of self-abuse have pallid, bloodless countenances, hollow, sunken and half-ghastly eyes, with a red rim around the eyelids, and black-and-blue semi-circles around the eyes. Red pimples on the face, with a black spot in their middles, are a sure sign of self-pollution in males, and irregularities in females. Stance is another sign: Self-polluters often stand and sit in the posture assumed during masturbation. They also often carry their hands to the private parts, and in laughing they throw this part of their bodies forward.

But are not the dangers exaggerated? That would be impossible! Masturbation poisons your body, breaks down your nerves, paralyses your whole system. When practised before puberty, it dwarfs and enfeebles the sexual organs. It also corrupts your morals and endangers your very soul's salvation. You may almost as well die outright as to thus pollute yourself.

Does it really lead to insanity? This excess causes more insanity than anything else except intemperance. Hundreds have been brought to our lunatic asylums by this single form of vice, and some must be tied down to prevent further destruction.

Ibid.

An even more interesting symptom was noted as late as 1954 by one eccentric Freudian psychiatrist:

Cf. the long, thin, almost imperceptible black hair growing out of the middle of the palm of the left hand of masturbators.

Rudolf Friedmann, 1954

The same gentleman touched upon a celebrated theological problem of sex:

In this connection one is reminded of Christ's constant aggression against his own mother deriving from the fact that his unconscious did not believe her to be a virgin.

Ibid.

Not everybody was so keen on abstention:

Though marriage has many pains, celibacy has no pleasures. The unmarried are outlaws of human nature. They are peevish at home and malevolent abroad. They dream away their time without friendship or fondness and are driven by boredom to childish

amusements or vicious delights. To live without feeling
or exciting sympathy, to be fortunate without adding to
the felicity of others ... is a state more gloomy than
solitude: it is not retreat but exclusion from mankind.

Samuel Johnson, *Rasselas*

We could fill numerous pages with the various foods and drinks
which supposedly encouraged (in rare cases, discouraged) sexual
activities. Seafood is supposedly aphrodisiac, possibly a deduction
from the legendary capabilities of sailors; hard and interestingly-
shaped objects like rhinoceros horns were, when powdered,
supposed to have a hardening effect on gentlemen. Lettuce, by the
same analogy, tended to produce limpness—though it should be
noted that (a) this does not work on rabbits, while (b) the ancient
Egyptians thought it had the opposite effect (perhaps a nice cool
lettuce is stimulating in the Nile heat, depressing in England).
Three favourites:

Wood pigeons check and blunt the manly powers; let
him not eat this bird who wishes to be amorous.

Martial (*c*.40–104AD), *Epigrams*

The immoderate use of chocolate in the seventeenth
century, was considered as so violent an inflamer of
the passions, that Joan. Fran. Rauch published a treatise
against it, and enforced the necessity of forbidding the
monks to drink it; and adds, that if such an interdiction
had existed, that scandal with which that holy order had
been branded might have proved more groundless.

Isaac Disraeli, *Curiosities of Literature*, 1791–3

White sugar is the curse of civilisation—it causes
fatigue and sexual apathy between husband and
wife. My recipe against sexual fatigue is to take honey in
large quantities; two Gev-E-Tabs, 10 vitamin E pills,
four wheatgerm oil tablets, four vitamin A pills, four
bonemeal tablets, six liver-plus tablets, two dessert-
spoons of Bio-Strath Elixir, twice a day.

Barbara Cartland

That last one sounds less like the advice of an experienced courtesan
than of a large shareholder in firms manufacturing Gev-E-Tabs,
Bio-Strath Elixir and the rest. Let us move hastily to a selection of

sexual oddities. First comes an Attorney-General, prosecuting a now-forgotten novel: the tone of moral outrage you must imagine for yourselves.

> The book deals with what everybody will recognise as an unsavoury subject—gratification of sexual appetite.

Sir Thomas Inskip, 1935

Naturally there could be only one result: the horrid work was banned for obscenity. In the hope of achieving this honour ourselves, we present a few little sexual quirks: Leather fetishism! A justification for rape! Bestiality! Xenophobia! And a new and awful motive for this whole sex business:

> I suggested to Himmler that he might dress two or three guard units in leather shorts. Obviously they would have to be handsome chaps, and not necessarily from the South. I can quite well imagine a soldier with a Hamburg accent displaying sunburnt knees.

Adolf Hitler, 1942

> Women resist in order to be conquered.

Ottavio Piccolomini (c.1600–1656)

> If only men could love each other like dogs, the world would be a paradise.

James Douglas, *Sunday Express*, 1930s

> This sort of thing may be tolerated by the French, but we are British—thank God.

Viscount Montgomery, on the Homosexuality Bill, 1965

> If paternity leave were granted it would result in a direct incitement to a population explosion.

Ian Gow MP, 1979

And an item which has us tensely waiting for 1986:

> I'll wager you that in 10 years it will be fashionable again to be a virgin.

Barbara Cartland, 1976

Spaceflight

Probably this chapter should be dedicated to Arthur C. Clarke—though his most celebrated prediction, that of the uses of communications satellites (in 1945!), was quite accurate, with the small and often regretted flaw that he failed to patent the notion. Clarke is a collector of mispredictions, and several plum items below (plus a few elsewhere, in our chapters on aviation and astronomy) are quoted in his books.

First we have an authoritative editorial statement from 1920.

S till, to be filled with uneasy wonder and to express it will be enough, for after the rocket quits our air and really starts on its longer journey, its flight would be neither accelerated nor maintained by the explosion of the charges it then might have left. To claim that it would be is to deny a fundamental law of dynamics, and only Dr Einstein and his chosen dozen, so few and fit, are licensed to do that.

That Professor Goddard, with his chair in Clark College and the countenancing of the Smithsonian Institution, does not know the relation of action to reaction, and of the need to have something better than a vacuum against which to react—to say that would be absurd. Of course he only seems to lack the knowledge ladled out daily in high schools.

But there are such things as intentional mistakes or oversights, and, as it happens, Jules Verne, who also knew a thing or two in assorted sciences—and had, besides, a surprising amount of prophetic power—deliberately seemed to make the same mistake that Professor Goddard seems to make. For the Frenchman, having got his travellers to or toward the moon into the desperate fix of riding a tiny satellite of the satellite, saved them from circling it forever by means of explosion, rocket fashion, where an explosion would not have had in the slightest degree the effect of releasing them from their dreadful slavery. That was one of

Verne's scientific slips, or else it was a deliberate step aside from scientific accuracy, pardonable enough in him as a romancer, but its like is not so easily explained when made by a savant who isn't writing a novel of adventure. **New York Times, 1920**

Motion in a vacuum (as science-fiction writer Bob Shaw puts it, 'Out there in the emptiness of space, what would Isaac Asimov have to push against?') is an old problem with an old solution to be found in Newton's Third Law of Motion: the editor of the *New York Times* had not considered that the exhaust from a rocket's jets has mass to 'react against'—the rocket! Jules Verne, likewise, is condemned for the good part of his science, whereas the silly part— the enormous cannon which shoots his ship into orbit and would incidentally crush the occupants into schnitzels—is overlooked. Verne was not happy when H. G. Wells used a more fanciful motive power:

I make use of physics. He [Wells] fabricates. I go to the moon in a cannon-ball discharged from a gun. There is no fabrication here. He goes to Mars in an airship which he constructs of a metal that does away with the laws of gravitation . . .

Jules Verne; but Wells' travellers went to the moon, not Mars

Back in reality, speculations on travel to the moon were being knocked about by scientists:

This foolish idea of shooting at the moon is an example of the absurd length to which vicious specialization will carry scientists working in thought-tight compartments. Let us critically examine the proposal. For a projectile entirely to escape the gravitation of the earth, it needs a velocity of 7 miles a second. The thermal energy of a gramme at this speed is 15,180 calories . . . The energy of our most violent explosive—nitroglycerine—is less than 1,500 calories per gramme. Consequently, even had the explosive nothing to carry, it has only one-tenth of the energy necessary to escape the earth . . . Hence the proposition appears to be basically impossible . . .

Professor A. W. Bickerton, 1926

As Clarke observes, violent explosives like nitroglycerine are fairly puny fuels: as pointed out by such as Tsiolkovski and Goddard years before, mixtures like kerosene/liquid oxygen contain much more energy for a given weight. Bickerton was thus fighting shadows.

Meanwhile, in Germany, Hermann Oberth had designed a World War I rocket which anticipated the V-2: this was rejected by the German War Ministry as fantasy. He wrote his PhD thesis on this rocket, and in 1922 the University of Heidelberg rejected it. He began to publish his theories, and Willy Ley records the immediate reaction of

> ... a series of articles attacking Oberth in a rather vehement manner. They were published in the very important journal of the VDI (*Verein Deutscher Ingenieure*, Society of German Engineers) and they were signed by Privy Councilor Professor Dr Lorenz of Danzig. Privy Councilor Lorenz did not make any elementary mistakes; he simply proved that Oberth's spaceship could not acquire the 'velocity of escape' of about seven miles per second. His arguments and calculation boiled down to the statement that a rocket fueled by known fuels, if it were to acquire that velocity, would have to weigh thirty-four times as much when fueled as it weighed when empty. The conclusion drawn from these calculations read: therefore it cannot be done.
>
> Oberth, naturally, wrote a reply. It was rejected. Dr Hohmann, being a member of the VDI as well as the VfR, also wrote a reply. It was rejected. The excuse given was lack of space. The real reason, which I learned through a personal conversation years later, was: 'We cannot permit people half his age to contradict the Privy Councilor!'
>
> **Willy Ley, *Rockets, Missiles and Space Travel*, 1951**

Later Oberth crushed Lorenz in debate by asking whether the Privy Councillor refused to believe the possibility of building a pot capable of holding thirty-four times its weight in water. No such successes were available in Britain:

> We follow with interest any work that is being done in other countries on jet propulsion, but scientific investigation into the possibilities has given no indi-

cation that this method can be a serious competitor to the airscrew-engine combination. We do not consider we should be justified in spending any time or money on it ourselves.

Reply from the Under-Secretary of State to the British Interplanetary Society, 1934

Even futurologists somehow seemed to miss the point:

The idea is that the flying machine will rise rapidly until it gets into the stratosphere, which is, approximately, fifteen miles above the earth. Once there its speed will be limited only by the capabilities of its structure. It would, in fact, stand still and allow the earth to revolve beneath it.

J. P. Lockhart-Mummery, *After Us*, 1936

The acceleration which must result from the use of rockets, or from being fired out of a gun by explosion, inevitably would damage the brain beyond repair. The exact rate of acceleration in feet per second that the human brain can survive is not known. It is almost certainly not enough, however, to render flight by rockets possible.

Ibid.

And, as with aviation, the astronomers were not exactly encouraging:

It must be said at once that the whole procedure sketched in the present volume presents difficulties of so fundamental a nature that we are forced to dismiss the notion as essentially impracticable, in spite of the author's insistent appeal to put aside prejudice and to recollect the supposed impossibility of heavier-than-air flight before it was actually accomplished. An analogy such as this may be misleading, and we believe it to be so in this case . . . .

Dr Richard Woolley, review in *Nature* of P. E. Cleator's *Rockets Through Space*, 1936

Twenty years later, in 1956, that very same reviewer was appointed Astronomer Royal. Asked by the press for his authoritative views on spaceflight, he said, 'Space travel is utter bilge.' Department of Excuses and Extenuations: Patrick Moore tells us that Woolley's celebrated reply was made under great stress, he having just arrived in England to take up the post of Astronomer Royal. Surrounded by rude and uncouth pressmen asking his views on absolutely everything, he was reduced to snap answers like 'Bilge!' to a good many questions.

In 1941 another distinguished astronomer, Professor J. W. Campbell of the University of Alberta, looked into the rocket problem and deduced that it would take one million tons of fuel to shift one pound of astronaut to the moon and back. In the event, this overestimated by a factor of about one million.

Next please:

B ut to place a man in a multi-stage rocket and project him into the controlling gravitational field of the moon, where the passenger can make scientific observations, perhaps land alive, and then return to earth—all that constitutes a wild dream worthy of Jules Verne.

Lee De Forest, the 'father of electronics', quoted in *Reader's Digest*, 1957

Even Patrick Moore, doyen of intelligent amateurs, published a paper in 1958 discussing the possibility of sending a rocket round the moon to photograph the hidden side. He said:

T o hope for an early success is being highly overoptimistic.

Depends what you mean by early. It took nearly fourteen months.

Sport

I make bold to say that I don't believe that in the future history of the world any such feat will be performed by anybody else.

Mayor of Dover to Matthew Webb after his English Channel swim, 1875

The Mayor is proved wrong each August when, on a calm day, fifteen or twenty people manage to swim the Channel—adding to the many hundreds who have done so over the intervening years, including children. However, this belief in the inviolability of sporting records and in certain unrepeatable feats was by no means new in 1875. The dizzy onward rush of new records and achievements in every type of sport since then should have acted as a warning against making such statements, but it has not.

Everybody loves to believe that the performance they have just watched will never be surpassed. The competitor's need is even greater—he must boost his own confidence by declaring himself eternally invincible. Also, so the theory goes, the more times you describe yourself as the best, the greater the number of people who will believe you—perhaps even your opponents. A good example is boxer Muhammad Ali, who has, over twenty years of victory and defeat, steadfastly declared himself to be 'the greatest', though occasionally he puts it slightly differently:

The man who will whip me will be fast, strong and hasn't yet been born.

And when the participants have such high opinions of themselves, how can the competition itself be any less over-emphasized?

I t will be the biggest commercial event in the history of the world.

Muhammad Ali again, on his \$25 million per man fight with Joe Frazier

I t will probably be the great sport event in history. Bigger than the Frazier—Ali fight. It really is the free world against the lying, cheating, hypocritical Russians.

Bobby Fischer on the world chess championship, 1972

I n this next fight, you are entering the greatest sporting competition of all time.

General Patton to American troops about to invade Sicily, 1943

One of the more dangerous of sports, that last one, though not so bad for the generals now that they no longer lead their men on to the field but can sit at home and watch the 'game' from the safety of their fall-out shelters.

And if war is just a sporting competition, some professional sports have most certainly become a type of warfare. Take soccer for example.

S ome people think football is a matter of life and death. I don't like that attitude. I can assure them it is much more serious than that.

Bill Shankly, soccer manager, 1973

T he growing gentleness of mankind will abolish, as barbarous, games which take the form of modified assault, as football, boxing, wrestling, fencing and the like.

T. Baron Russell, *A Hundred Years Hence*, 1905

[Soccer] is one of the biggest things that's happened in creation—bigger than any 'ism' you can name.

Alan Brown, soccer manager, 1968

Ah, yes, sport has become so big and important that winning is everything and

N ice guys finish last.

Leo Durocher, baseball manager, 1946

The other major sporting fallacy is that nothing will change, that new ideas will never catch on and can safely be ridiculed.

J ust a fad. A passing fancy.

Phil Wrigley, baseball owner, on night games

Nowadays many outdoor sports are played in the evenings under floodlights—even cricket!—on the premise that attendances, and thus gate receipts, will be greater. The accent is on money.

W hat we have here is the Mona Lisa. You expect us to sell it for chopped liver?

Jerry Perenchio, US boxing promoter, on the Frazier–Ali fight, 1971

F ootball doesn't pay much.

Johann Cruyff, Dutch soccer star, after signing a £290,000 seven-year contract, 1973

All this dreadful commercialism makes one nostalgic for the old days, for the old ideas on sport:

W eekend football is the best training for a player. If you put him to hard work on weekdays you make him stale and listless.

John Goodall, soccer player, c.1880

F ox-hunting will never die. The need for it is there, and what has sprung out of the loins of one's ancestors will be promulgated to future generations.

Major Vivian Nickells, *Oats, Wars and Horses*, 1932

C amels is a fighting man's cigarette ... gives you that extra round!

Floyd Patterson, world heavyweight boxing champion, 1961

... and no doubt gives you that extra cough in the mornings, too. Ah, they don't make advertisements like that any more.
  Let us turn, now, to the question of intelligence in sport ...

A high degree of skill and intelligence are required [for croquet] and therefore it is not going to attract the lower income groups.

Chairman of the Croquet Association, c.1970

Football has become so complicated that the student will find it a recreation to go to classes.

T. S. Eliot

In the future, amusements will be intelligent and educational, games of brute strength will die out and there will be new games of mental skill. Boxers, footballers, and others who rely mainly upon their strength for a living will be regarded as 'throw outs' of low mental capacity.

A. M. Low, *The Future*, 1925

That last one sounds almost slanderous. And what do the fine, intelligent members of the boxing profession have to say in their own defence?

This boy Cotton could beat three-thirds of the light-heavies around today, and with a little more experience he'll do even better than that.

Whitey Bimstein, boxing trainer, 1961

So much for professionalism. But what of amateur sport?

The Olympic movement appears as a ray of sunshine through clouds of racial animosity, religious bigotry and political chicanery.

Avery Brundage, President, International Olympic Committee, 1972

The Americans ought to be ashamed of themselves for letting their medals be won by Negroes.

Adolf Hitler, after the Berlin Olympics, 1936

The Olympic Games can no more have a deficit than a man can have a baby.

Mayor Jean Drapeau of Montreal, just before the disastrously expensive 1976 Montreal Olympics

And, while on the subject of babies:

T he 880-yard heel and toe walk is the closest a man can come to experiencing the pangs of childbirth.

Avery Brundage again, 1956

One does wonder just how he can be so certain about it.

Transport

I f a man were to propose to convey us regularly to
Edinburgh [by stage-coach] in seven days, and bring
us back in seven more, should we not vote him to
Bedlam?

Sir Henry Herbert MP, 1671

The perils of modern high-speed travel, from the stage-coach to
Concorde, have always been a prolific source of alarm and
despondency. Again and again pundits have declared that people's
brains would explode if conveyed at more than three miles per hour,
or some such figure. This follows a confusion of high speed
(harmless in itself, though protection from wind is advisable) with
high acceleration/deceleration. Astronauts can accelerate to
enormous speeds by doing it gradually; motorists can kill
themselves by rapid deceleration from a mere twenty-five miles per
hour, as caused by the efficient braking power of a brick wall.
Another stage-coach example concerns

> a local physician who wrote in the *Bath Argus* in the 18th
> century to warn us of the perils of modern high-speed
> travel. In the 1780s John Palmer had introduced the
> mail coach, carrying also a few passenges at a higher fare
> than that charged by the existing 'slow coaches', and had
> thereby reduced the time between London and Bath
> from 3 days to a mere 17 hours. The good doctor
> deplored such unnatural speed and solemnly warned
> that if the trend continued we should all die of apoplexy.
>
> **The Times letter, 1980**

The hideous prospects of eighteenth-century jet lag were as nothing
to the doom-laden comments on the next century's railway
enthusiasm:

> I am sorry to find the intelligent people of the North
> country gone mad on the subject of railways.
>
> **Lord Eldon, c.1815**

What can be more palpably absurd and ridiculous than the prospect held out of locomotives travelling *twice as fast* as stage-coaches! We should as soon expect the people of Woolwich to suffer themselves to be fired off upon one of Congreve's ricochet rockets, as trust themselves to the mercy of such a machine going at such a rate ... We trust that Parliament will, in all railways it may sanction, limit the speed to *eight or nine miles per hour*, which we entirely agree ... is as great as can be ventured on with safety.

*Quarterly Review, c.*1825

In 1825 a Parliamentary committee sat on George Stephenson's proposal for a Liverpool–Manchester railway: denunciations of Stephenson and his plan came thick and fast:

Every part of the scheme shows that this man has applied himself to a subject of which he has no knowledge, and to which he has no science to apply.

These locomotive engines will be a terrible nuisance in consequence of the fire and smoke vomited forth by them.

The value of land in the neighbourhood of Manchester alone would be deteriorated by no less than £20,000!

Various quotations from the proceedings and press

The most absurd scheme that ever entered into the head of man to conceive.

Mr Alderson, a leading counsel

[The locomotive is] in direct opposition both to the law of God and to the most enduring interests of society.

Declaration of a meeting of Manchester ministers

In this year, too, although we have not been able to track down the author paraphrased by Fuller, someone unaware of a decade's successful railway operations went so far as to say that:

The weight of the locomotive would completely prevent its moving and that railways, even if made, could *never* be worked by steam power.

J. F. C. Fuller, *Pegasus or the Future of Transport*, c.1926

More contemporary prophecies of equal validity were as follows:

The doctors declared that the air would be poisoned and birds would die of suffocation. The landowners, that the preservation of pheasants and foxes was no longer possible. Householders, that their houses would be burnt down and the air polluted by clouds of smoke. Horsebreeders, that horses would become extinct. Farmers, that oats and hay would be rendered unsaleable. Innkeepers, that inns would be ruined. Passengers, that boilers would burst. Heaven knows who—'that the locomotive would prevent cows grazing, hens laying, and would cause ladies to give premature birth to children at the sight of these things moving at four and a half miles an hour!'

Fuller, *ibid*.

You are entering upon an enormous undertaking of which you know nothing. Then look at the recklessness of your proceedings! You are proposing to destroy property, cutting up our estates in all directions! Why, gentlemen, if this sort of thing be permitted to go on, you will in a very few years *destroy the noblesse*!

Sir Astley Cooper, eminent surgeon and MP, on the Birmingham railway bill

America was less worried about the nobs, but also (uncharacteristically early) had qualms about the environment. One pundit was only eight years away from becoming US President when he wrote:

As you well know, Mr President, railroad carriages are pulled at the enormous speed of 15mph, by 'engines' which in addition to endangering life and limb of passengers, roar and snort their way through the countryside, setting fire to the crops, scaring the livestock and frightening women and children. The Almighty certainly never intended that people should travel at such breakneck speed.

Martin Van Buren, then Governor of New York, letter to President Andrew Jackson, 1829

By 1841, with the railway boom still increasing, Stephenson himself had an attack of caution. Despite having built an engine capable of running at eighty miles per hour, he decided:

I should say no railway ought to exceed 40 miles an hour on the most favourable gradient; but on a curved line the speed ought not to exceed 24 or 25 miles an hour.

Perhaps British Rail are merely obeying Stephenson's dictum when their services somehow fail to reach the promised 125mph. Our last item on rail travel is an accurate prediction of smoker carriages and ventilation in general:

Rail travel at high speed is not possible, because passengers, unable to breathe, would die of asphyxia.

Dr Dionysius Lardner

But the Reverend Dr Lardner is most celebrated for being wrong about steamships. In this he was in good company. When, in 1803, Napoleon Bonaparte was planning to invade Britain from Boulogne, he was approached by the American engineer Robert Fulton, who explained how the British Fleet could be defeated—by using steam-powered ships. The Little Corporal was somewhat less than enthusiastic about the suggestion:

What, sir, you would make a ship sail against the wind and currents by lighting a bonfire under her decks? I pray you excuse me. I have no time to listen to such nonsense.

It was in 1836–8 that Dr Lardner's fulminations against steamships reached their peak. By complex calculations he proved to his own satisfaction that the 2,800 to 4,500-mile journey across the Atlantic was impossible for such vessels:

W e have, as an extreme limit of a steamer's practical voyage, without receiving a relay of coals, a run of about 2,000 miles.

When the eminent physicist Joseph Henry visited the British Association meeting in Liverpool in this period, Lardner rudely refused to believe Henry's mild claim to have travelled 150 miles by water (Albany to New York) in nine hours: steamboats, Lardner knew, could never sustain a speed of even fifteen miles per hour so Henry's story was transparent nonsense. The final distillation of his wisdom was:

M en might as well project a voyage to the moon as attempt to employ steam across the stormy North Atlantic.

Address to the British Association, 1838, quoted in Patrick Moore's *Space in the Sixties*

By 1875 the focus of controversy was what the US Congressional Record termed the 'so-called internal combustion engine'.

T he dangers are obvious. Stores of gasoline in the hands of the people interested primarily in profit would constitute a fire and explosive hazard of the first rank. Horseless carriages propelled by gasoline engines might attain speeds of 14 or even 20 miles per hour. The menace to our people of vehicles hurtling through our streets and along our roads poisoning the atmosphere would call for prompt legislative action even if the military and economic implications were not so over-whelming. The Secretary of War has testified before us and has pointed out the destructive effects of the use of such vehicles in battle. Furthermore, the supplies of petroleum, from which gasoline can be extracted only in limited quantities, make it imperative that the defence forces should have first call on the limited supply. Furthermore, the cost of producing it is far beyond the financial capacity of private industry, yet the safety of the nation demands that an adequate supply should be produced. In addition, the development of this new power may displace the use of horses, which would wreck our agriculture.

... The discovery with which we are dealing involves forces of a nature too dangerous to fit into any of our usual concepts.

US Congressional Record, 1875

It was a while before anyone took the automobile seriously. The astute US businessman Chauncey Depew confessed that he warned his nephew not to invest $5,000 in Henry Ford's company because

N othing has come along that can beat the horse and buggy.

Speaking of horses and buggies, we were unable to track down the prophet of doom (or optimistic rose-grower) who allegedly warned that, if New York's traffic problem continued to increase, by 1920 the whole city would be four feet deep in horse manure. Also elusive is the

... long forgotten spokesman for Daimler Benz who said that there would never be a mass market for motor cars —about 1,000 in Europe—because that was the limit on the number of chauffeurs available!

Public Finance and Accountancy, Nov. 1979

But by now the focus of misprediction had shifted to aviation and even space travel, and to prevent this chapter from getting completely out of hand we have dealt with these topics separately.

Meanwhile we offer an all-purpose argument for travel abroad by any means whatever—courtesy of

M ikhail Suslov, the veteran Politburo ideologue, who is reported to have remarked once that he could not see what there could possibly be of interest abroad when there was everything one wanted within the Soviet Union.

The Times, 11 July 1980

Ah, if only we had the good luck to live in the Soviet Union.

Warfare

A nd ye shall hear of wars and rumours of wars ...
Nation shall rise against nation and kingdom against
kingdom: and there shall be famines, and pestilences.

Matthew, xxiv

This is a highly reliable all-purpose prediction, and since its
utterance there can have been few times when it was not entirely
justified by event. Persons since Christ have often chosen their
words less carefully when laying down the law on warfare:

I will ignore all ideas for new works and engines of war,
the invention of which has reached its limits and for
whose improvement I see no further hope.

**Julius Frontinus, Emperor Vespasian's leading military
engineer, first century AD**

Even war preparations have not always been wholly sensible; we
find that, on the news of World War I mobilization, the first task of
the British Army's armourers was to sharpen the officer's swords
for battle. A Civil Service job created in 1803 required its holder to
lurk on the cliffs of Dover with a spyglass, his duty to ring a bell
should he see Napoleon coming: this post was abolished in 1945.
More forward-looking was Winston Churchill who, with his War
Cabinet, considered having icebergs towed down from the Arctic
for use as floating airstrips during the assault on Europe. (This was
'Project Habbakuk': one of its advantages was that bomb craters in
these airstrips could swiftly be filled with water, which would freeze
flat.)

In fact the spyglass on the cliffs of Dover had been anticipated
and improved upon back in the thirteenth century, by that foremost
scientist of the time (in so far as there *were* any scientists in the
Christian world just then), Roger Bacon. He claimed that Julius
Caesar had 'erected very large mirrors in order that he might see in
advance from the shores of Gaul the arrangement of the cities and
camps of England', and suggested that 'similar mirrors might be
erected on an elevation opposite hostile cities and armies, so that all
that was being done by the enemy might be visible'.

Mirrors were reportedly put to still more effective use by Archimedes during the defence of Syracuse, to concentrate sunlight upon enemy ships and set them ablaze—quite a cunning weapon if you can persuade said enemy to stay still at a few yards' range while you focus several dozen mirrors on his ship.

What have this century's prophets said about warfare?

The idea that cavalry will be replaced by these iron coaches is absurd. It is little short of treasonous.

ADC to Field Marshal Haig, watching a tank demonstration,
1916

In the future, massive floating forts will take the place of our present battleships; these will be able to constantly move their positions, probably under cover of artificial fogs ... Huge submarines will bring armoured tanks to within, say, a mile of the shores of any country, where they would be disgorged and quickly run to dry land ... There will naturally be great activity in the air. Huge aeroplanes, launched by compressed air, will convey loads of men and apparatus readily to any point ...

A. M. Low, *The Future*, 1925

In the future the applications of science will further ameliorate the hardships of the combatant soldier. It is strange, however, that the activities of the League of Nations have temporarily prevented any advance being made in that application of science which most promised an increased humanity in warfare. I refer, of course, to the League's prohibition of the use of gases as weapons. It is certain that in the near future chemists could have produced a gas capable of causing prolonged insensibility with no harmful after-effects. The introduction of such gases (or clouds of vesicant particles) would obviously revolutionize warfare. It might conceivably make battles, as we understand them, impossible.

Earl of Birkenhead, *The World in 2030*, 1930

Possibly within the next hundred years military airplanes, propelled by some form of atomic energy, will become common. Such machines will be able to remain in the air for an indefinite period, so long as they are provided with food for their occupants. A fleet of these airplanes might blockade a frontier or overawe a capital as effectively as a fleet of warships . . .

Ibid.

Thus all arms, except the air, will be reduced to tanks of various descriptions, each designed to fulfil some special function. Such a development has, of course, as its goal the theoretically perfect war-machine, a submersible battleship capable also of flying in the air and travelling across the land. Though many will deride this conception as fantastic, its attainment is certainly not to be lightly dismissed . . .

Ibid.

We need hardly comment on the above. Getting it right does little for one's short-term reputation, either. The machine-gun's inventor must have been properly mortified by Field Marshal Haig's description of it as 'A grossly overrated weapon'—though some half-million people in the Field-Marshal's own war and quite a few more since have reason to disbelieve him. In 1914 Sir Arthur Conan Doyle published his story 'Danger!' predicting the submarine blockade of England, and official response was swift:

Most improbable and more like one of Jules Verne's stories.

Admiral Sir Compton Dombile

A more detailed rebuttal came from Admiral William Hannan Henderson, who strenuously objected to the prophecy

. . . that territorial waters will be violated, or neutral vessels sunk. Such will be absolutely prohibited, and will only recoil on the heads of the perpetrators. No nation would permit it, and the officer who did it would be shot.

Within a few months of the story's appearance and the above pronouncements, a German submarine blockade was announced.

World War II produced some still more interesting comments, including one which makes us wonder who, after all, started it:

> I think it's pretty obvious that this war is no pleasure for me. For five years I have been separated from the rest of the world. I haven't been to the theatre, I haven't heard a concert, and I haven't seen a movie.
>
> **Adolf Hitler**

Neither did the Americans have anything to do with it:

> I have told you once and I tell you again—your boys will not be sent into any foreign wars.
>
> **Franklin D. Roosevelt, election speech, 1940**

And of course the usual optimism came welling up:

> In three weeks England will have her neck wrung like a chicken.
>
> **General Weygand, on the fall of France.**
> **Churchill said: 'Some chicken, some neck!'**

> Defeat of Germany means the defeat of Japan, probably without firing a shot or losing a life.
>
> **Franklin D. Roosevelt**

> For the good of the German people, we must wish for a war every fifteen or twenty years.
>
> **Hitler, 1941**

The atomic bomb was of course the biggest talking-point; it had been predicted by H. G. Wells (in *The World Set Free*: but Wells felt that such a bomb would keep on going off, emitting lava and unpleasantness for days or weeks on end) and therefore was not taken too seriously—though some put-downs of the idea in Congress and the House of Commons were for reasons of security rather than disbelief. Not, however, the following:

A tomic energy might be as good as our present day explosives, but it is unlikely to produce anything very much more dangerous.

Churchill, 1939

There has been a great deal said about a 3,000 miles high-angle rocket. In my opinion such a thing is impossible for many years. The people who have been writing these things that annoy me, have been talking about a 3,000 miles high-angle rocket shot from one continent to another, carrying an atomic bomb and so directed as to be a precise weapon which would land exactly on a certain target, such as a city.

I say, technically, I don't think anyone in the world knows how to do such a thing, and I feel confident that it will not be done for a very long period of time to come ... I think we can leave that out of our thinking. I wish the American public would leave that out of their thinking.

Dr Vannevar Bush, 1945

That is the biggest fool thing we have ever done. The bomb will never go off, and I speak as an expert in explosives.

Admiral William Leahy to President Truman, 1945

The most popular war prediction is, of course, that leitmotif of Lord Beaverbrook's press throughout the 1930s: THERE WILL BE NO WAR.

This man Churchill is the enemy of the British Empire ... This man Churchill is a warmonger. He is turning the thoughts of the British Empire to war. He must be stopped.

Lord Beaverbrook, 1939, quoted by Patrick Campbell

(By this time H. G. Wells was bitterly regretting his coinage of the phrase 'the war to end war'.) Beaverbrook's no-war prophecies were intended to be self-fulfilling; the more orthodox reason given for this unlikely prospect is that the sheer destructive power of modern weaponry makes war too hideous to be envisaged (as can of course be seen from the total lack of bloodshed worldwide since

6 August, 1945). Unfortunately, even after Hiroshima, a certain military body went on to envisage Nagasaki.

> G unpowder and military machinery have rendered the triumph of barbarians impossible. Steam has united nations in the closest bonds.
>
> **William E. Lecky (1838–1903)**

> T he nuclear arms race has no military purpose. Wars cannot be fought with nuclear weapons.
>
> **Earl Mountbatten, May 1979—a statement which may yet be disproved**

> T here will one day spring free from the brain of science a machine or force so fearful in its potentialities, so absolutely terrifying that even man, the fighter, who will dare torture and death in order to inflict torture and death, will be appalled, and so abandon war forever. What man's mind can create, man's character can control.
>
> **Thomas Alva Edison**

We can, however, conclude on two notes of hope:

> I f Hitler were alive today, the German girls wouldn't let him bomb London if the Beatles were there.
>
> **Anonymous, c. 1965**

Flower power, anyone?

> I seriously doubt if we will have another war. This [Vietnam] is probably the last.
>
> **Richard Nixon, 1971**

Women

Were there no women, men might live like gods.

Edward Douwes Dekker

One wonders what gods Dekker was considering: perhaps the austere, navel-contemplating variety, perhaps the blood-and-wine Valhallans ... certainly not those who, like Zeus, had other enthusiasms. The sentiment, though, is not uncommon. Women have always had a bad press, ascribable to the fact that scribes were monks and monks were men—men told several times a day that women were nothing but monstrous temptations. (Categorical remarks about the awfulness of males had to wait for the feminist movement.) More inside facts follow below ...

A garrulous, deceitful thing is woman.

Tasso

Woman are one and all a set of vultures.

Petronius

The fundamental fault of the female character is that it has no sense of justice.

Arthur Schopenhauer (1788–1860)

The perfect woman, who obviously does not exist, is gentle, unaffected, liberal-minded and non-predatory.

Sidney Coe Howard

This last item hints at the womanly ideal. When not indulging in her usual pastimes of being garrulous, deceitful, vulture-like, unjust, harsh, affected, illiberal and predatory, a woman should strive to be a cuddly little chattel. She should be seen but not heard. She should, if possible, be helpless (though not, of course, to the extent of being unable to wait hand and foot on her man). This is the way God wants it:

God made the woman for the use of man.

Tennyson

Silence and modesty are the best ornaments of women.

Euripides

A woman will bear any weight, if it's placed upon her by a man.

Aristophanes

There is no woman but she will yield in time.

John Lyly

A woman is a solitary, helpless creature without a man.

Thomas Shadwell

Women were created for the comfort of men.

James Howell

In the highest society, as well as in the lowest, woman is merely an instrument of pleasure.

Leo Tolstoy

That last remark of Tolstoy's means, presumably, that the high- or low-society woman is expected to dress nicely, wear make-up and perfume to taste, and in general comport herself as befits a well-tuned instrument of pleasure. It thus seems a bit unfair to catch her on the rebound with this austere remark:

The whole trade in the luxuries of life is brought into existence and supported by the requirements of women.

Leo Tolstoy

After all, being an instrument of pleasure is the lady's life-work:

A woman is happy and attains all that she deserves when she captivates a man; hence the great object of her life is to master the art of captivating men.

Leo Tolstoy

Luckily much advice is available on how she should make the most of her charms—in the most modest and unaffected of ways:

Every well-sexed woman invariably throws her shoulders back and breasts forward as if she would render them conspicuous, and further signifies sensuality by way of a definite rolling motion of the posterior.

Orson Squire Fowler, *Sexual Science,* **1870**

After lengthy observational research we are forced to concede that such throwing and rolling are *occasionally* practised, though we were unable to ascertain how well sexed the practitioners were.
But peril lurks!

All well-sexed maidens enter womanhood with a plump, luscious bust, which usually shrivels gradually till it almost disappears by age twenty.

Ibid.

The truth is inescapable—all those plumply luscious maidens of twenty-one or more are guilty of some artful deception. Let us not be too harsh: this is merely because their greatest goal is to become wives and mothers:

The charge that women do not wish to become mothers is one of the greatest of many gross and unfair libels which women have had to endure in silence. They are the few and unnatural who would not prefer this normal privilege of womankind.

Lydia E. Pinkham, *Private Textbook Upon Ailments Peculiar to Women*

When I come to power, I promise you, every German girl shall get a German husband.

Adolf Hitler

Luckily men are always ready to cater to these needs, sometimes with disarming enthusiasm:

W̶e all live in polygamy, *at least* for a time and usually for good. Since every man needs many women, there could be nothing more just than that he should be free, indeed obliged, to support many women. This would also mean the restoration of woman to her rightful and natural position, the subordinate one.

Arthur Schopenhauer

A̶ vast body of research 'proved'—to no-one's great surprise—that if the ethnic groups were ordered in terms of their distance up the ladder of evolution, white Anglo-Saxon Protestants would be in the lead, followed by Northern Europeans, Slavs, Jews, Italians, and so on, with Negroes trailing in the far rear. By the 1860s natural scientists could pinpoint women's place on the evolutionary ladder with some precision—she was at the level of the Negro.

Barbara Ehrenreich & Deirdre English, *For Her Own Good: 150 Years of the Experts' Advice to Women*, **1979**

And of course women's natural purity would preserve them from anything dubious in the way of sex. The British Parliament did indeed include lesbianism among the many things forbidden by an Act passed in Queen Victoria's day, but the Queen herself refused to believe or even to consider that women could be involved in such unparliamentary acts, and the offending passage was discreetly removed. Thus for many years male but not female homosexuality was punishable in British law.

This brings us to the struggle between the sexes. From the nineteenth century until late in the twentieth, the general consensus was that women were pretty feeble things.

I̶f woman should become the serious rival of man in many branches of industry, she would, as the weaker, be crushed without consideration. Gallantry is an invention of prosperity and leisure.

Max Nordau

A woman's mind isn't trained like ours. She couldn't take those decisions, no. The female mind will not work that fast. The female mind will not have the intestinal fortitude to stand up to the guff the players would give them. And when I say intestinal fortitude, I mean a four-letter word called guts.

Chris Pelekondas, former baseball umpire, on the question of women umpires, 1976

On the other hand, sporting questions made it essential to keep women in their place since, horror of horrors, they might accidentally fail to be inferior:

There is the possibility that a boy could be beaten by a girl and as a result be ashamed to face his family and friends. I wonder if anybody has stopped to think what that could do to a young boy?

Charlie Maas, Indiana State Coaches Association, on proposals for mixed sports, 1974

Athletic competition builds character in our boys. We do not need that kind of character in our girls.

American judge ruling against a girl athlete excluded from a school team on sex grounds, 1973

Probably the judge had in mind the foul-mouthed and brutally domineering woman implied in the next two sayings:

The language down the pit is no worse than in a ladies' shoe shop.

Tom Lindop, member of the Newcastle-under-Lyme Industrial Tribunal, 1979.

Why should a married woman want a mortgage in her own name? We'll have husbands doing the housework next.

Eric Nash, branch manager, Magnet & Planet Building Society, 1976

Legally, too, no chances were taken for a long time:

S ir, nature has given woman so much power that the law cannot afford to give her more.

Samuel Johnson

On the intellectual front, no hint of equality was to be tolerated: a fairly standard proof of inferiority follows:

T he knowledge of all knowledge, philosophy, is a masculine domain. Women can learn and understand philosophical ideas, and even act according to them. But they cannot conceive ideas of decisive significance and effect in this field. For this reason all great thinkers, philosophers and founders of religions were men, and so it will remain. If a woman is exceptionally successful in one of these fields of learning, then there is something wrong with her sex hormones.

Oscar Kiss Maerth, *The Beginning Was the End*, trans. 1973

In condensed form, this argument can be phrased: All ladies are deficient. If they are not deficient they are not ladies. This proves it. To prove it still more rigorously by independent authority:

W hen a woman becomes a scholar there is usually something wrong with her sexual organs.

Nietzsche

The chorus continues:

W omen love us for our defects; if we have enough of them they will forgive us even our superior intellects.

Oscar Wilde

T he nobler and more perfect a thing is, the later and more slowly does it mature. The man attains the maturity of his reasoning powers and spiritual faculties hardly before his twenty-eighth year; the woman with her eighteenth. And then it is only reasoning power of a sort: a very limited sort. Thus women remain children all their lives, never see anything but what is closest to them, cleave to the present moment, take appearance for reality and prefer trifles to the most important affairs.

Arthur Schopenhauer

W omen never reason, and therefore they are (comparatively) seldom wrong. They judge instinctively of what falls under their immediate observation or experience, and do not trouble themselves about remote or doubtful consequences. If they make no profound discoveries, they do not involve themselves in gross absurdities.

William Hazlitt, *Characteristics*, 1823

Would these opinions, we ask ourselves, stand up in court? Well:

T he woman barrister looks and is ridiculous; and has been so since Portia. Neither should the sex sit on juries; no woman will believe that a witness wearing the wrong hat can be giving the right evidence.

James Agate, *Ego 6*, 1944

A ll Berkshire women are very silly. I don't know why women in Berkshire are more silly than anywhere else.

Judge Claude Duveen, Reading County Court, 1972

Women, in short, should stick to supporting the trade in the luxuries of life—specifically, clothes.

T here is not gown or garment that worse becomes a woman than when she will be wise.

Luther

T he only thing that has been taught successfully to women is to wear becomingly the fig-leaf they received from their first mother.

Denis Diderot

Speaking of fig-leaves brings us with suspicious neatness to the consolations of religion. Surely religion, excepting the odd demented Ayatollah, has words of comfort for the women it won't allow to become priests? Indeed yes:

As regards the individual nature, woman is defective and misbegotten.

St Thomas Aquinas

The female sex is in some respects inferior to the male sex, both as regards body and soul.

The Catholic Encyclopaedia, c. 1940

However, the following deduction from Scripture is probably not officially endorsed by the Vatican:

The Bible says that woman is the last thing which God made. He must have made it on Saturday night. It shows fatigue.

Alexandre Dumas

It took the acute observation of an Archbishop to bring us our final and theologically rigorous condemnation of womankind.

Woman is a creature without reason who pokes the fire from the top.

Archbishop Whately

World's End

Armageddon, the Day of Judgement, the Second Coming and such-like small events have always been a staple diet of the prophets. Here is a list of popular years which were expected to mark the end, or in certain cases the beginning, of the somewhat protracted end.

195AD This was deduced by numerology from the Greek spelling of Rome and the Greek value of its letters: *rho* (100), *omega* (800), *mu* (40), *eta* (8). These add up to 948, which must therefore be the number of years Rome would last. Founded in 753BC, it must fall in 195AD, and the rest of the world would naturally follow.

365AD Known for obvious reasons as the Year of Days, this seemed a numerologically likely Last Year. When Armageddon failed to occur, one would have expected people to leap (as it were) to the conclusion that 366 was in with a chance; but leap years had been established—with the Julian calendar—only in 46BC, and were perhaps looked on as new-fangled.

1000 Chapter *xx* of the Book of *Revelation* refers to the 'millennium' . . .

1030 Possibly the thousand years were to be measured from the Passion rather than the Nativity.

1033 As for 1030.

1492 Sir Thomas Browne (in *Pseudodoxia Epidemica*) noted the beliefs that (a) the world was created in 5509BC, and (b) its ordained lifetime was 7,000 years. Writing in 1645, Browne detected a possible incompatibility.

1496 This year received the astrological seal of approval from several quarters—and by way of solid proof, a monster was reportedly fished from the Tiber early in the year (it had a donkey's head, maiden's body, stag's right foot, griffin's left foot and a wizened face where its rump should be).

1524 (February) This was chosen by the astrologer Stoffler, who calculated that Saturn, Mars and Jupiter would be together in the sign of Pisces, inevitably heralding a worldwide flood. At least one ark was constructed, but through lack of water failed to get off the ground.

1588 Stoffler's second try:

> H ostile contemporaries, with a sneer, note 1588 as unusually barren of happenings; surely an exaggeration, for the waters covered, if not the earth, at least the Great Armada.
>
> **Geoffrey Dennis, *The End of the World*, 1930**

1666 The vague connection with the Number of the Beast was enough to make this a sinister year (people seemed less worried about 666AD); again God misfired, and merely destroyed London in the Great Fire.

1833 This was the first attempt of the prolific doomster William Miller, who favoured elaborate numerological calculations based on the books of *Daniel* and *Revelation*. In addition, Miller was in direct contact with God, who obliged to the extent of a spectacular meteor-shower.

1834 If the world didn't end in 1833 it could not fail (said Miller) to do so in 1834, at the latest.

1843 (21 March, midnight) Miller recalculated furiously after 1834's lack of fiasco, and presumably found he had transposed a couple of digits. One of the five new proofs ran as follows. From *Leviticus xxvi*, the Israelites were to be punished 'seven times' for their sins, meaning seven 'years' of 360 days, giving 2520 days. Merely subtract the date of the first captivity in Babylon (677BC), and the answer is 1843! The other four calculations are a little less irrefutably convincing than this. Miller was rewarded this time with a comet.

1844 (21 March, midnight) Miller's absolutely definite final date. When nothing happened, his disciples fragmented and despondently became—among other things—Seventh Day Adventists.

1847 Predicted by one Harriet Livermore for inscrutable reasons; Joseph Wolff (1795–1865), the missionary, also deduced this date—from the prophecies of Daniel. For other Daniel-powered predictions, see 1833, 1834, 1843 and 1844.

1874 Cleverly predicted *after the event* by Charles Taze Russell, whose sect later became the Jehovah's Witnesses. Study of the Bible and the Great Pyramid informed him that the Second Coming had in fact happened this year, but nobody had noticed; after forty years of lurking incognito, Christ would get busy and annihilate everyone who failed to join Russell's church.

1881

> The world then to an end shall come
> In Eighteen Hundred and Eighty-One
>
> **_Life and Prophecies of Ursula Sontheil_, better known as Mother Shipton**

1882 When Mother Shipton's prediction for 1881 failed, it was realized that her couplet had been misread. There had been an error in translation from the English. What it *should* have said was:

> The world then at an end we'll view
> In Eighteen Hundred and Eighty-Two.

When this prediction failed it was realized that ... but see under 1991.

1911 Charles Piazzi Smyth, Astronomer-Royal of Scotland, had published his monumental *Our Inheritance in the Great Pyramid* (1864), which like the rehabilitated Mother Shipton picked on 1882—not for the End but for the beginning of the period of tribulation preceding the Second Coming in 1911. This was because the length of the Pyramid's 'Grand Gallery', measured in pyramid inches (1.0011 inches each), yields either 1882 or 1911 depending on how you measure it.

1914 Charles Taze Russell's year of doom (see under 1874). Rather than be consoled by having accidentally predicted the First World War, Russell's followers were so unsporting as to alter his Pyramidological book here and there:

> The deliverance of the saints must take place some time before 1914 ...
>
> **Russell, *Studies in the Scripture*, vol III, 1910 ed.**

The deliverance of the saints must take place very soon after 1914 . . .

Ibid., **1923 ed.**

1917 More study of *Revelation*, mingled with the Number of the Beast—now identified as Kaiser Wilhelm—gave this ineffectual date.

1920 Another Pyramid prediction, this time from Colonel J. Garnier (1905).

1921 (April), and *1924* These were calculated from the Book of *Daniel*, the Great Pyramid yet again, and even more obscure calculations involving the downfall of the Catholic Church and the final conversion of the Jews.

1925 The choice of Judge J. F. Rutherford, an early Jehovah's Witness. Rather than recalculate, he fell discreetly silent when nothing happened: since this time, the sect has kept quiet about the date of the Millennium (apart from hints that it won't be long).

1928 (29 May) The final war was to begin at this time, again by decree of the Great Pyramid:

The Pyramid symbolism, when considered in conjunction with Biblical prophecy, indicates that its message is addressed to the present era, and that the final Time of Tribulation, so often prophesied in the Bible, is now upon us.

D. Davidson & H. Aldersmith, *The Great Pyramid: Its Divine Message*, **1924**

It has been a long, hard tribulation.

1931 Heavily tipped by the Prophetical Society of Dallas, Texas—at least up to approximately 1930.

1936 (6 September) Originally noted as the final year in *The Great Pyramid: Its Divine Message* (see 1928), this year was also plugged by one George F. Riffert, who was slightly at a loss when little happened:

A very real problem was, and still is, to ascertain the literal significance and character of the epoch whose crisis date was September 6, 1936.

Riffert, *Great Pyramid Proof of God*, editions after 1936

Finally he decided that King Edward VIII's decision to abdicate was the cosmic event the Pyramid was built to foretell.

195? (21 December) The choice of 'Mrs Marian Keech', whose information came *via* automatic writing from flying saucers. Atlantis and Mu would rise as America sank, and flying saucers would ferry the elect to safety.

1953 (20 August) The date of the Second Coming to be found in the revised (1940) edition of *The Great Pyramid: Its Divine Message*. Christ was scheduled to smite all but the Anglo-Saxons (the 'true Israel'). The Anglo-Israelite sect subsequently explained that the New Age had indeed begun that day, though not in a manner perceptible to unbelievers.

1969 Charles Manson expected a race Armageddon to begin this year, and planned to touch it off by a little murdering of his own.

1972 (7 January) The choice of Herbert W. Armstrong, publisher of the fundamentalist magazine *The Plain Truth*. He believed in nineteen-year cycles; he first started broadcasting his views to the USA in 1934 and to Europe in 1953, so inevitably 1972 must see the millennium. Afterwards Armstrong explained:

Moses made mistakes, Abraham made mistakes, David made mistakes, Elijah made mistakes ...

1973 One interpretation of Nostradamus has Armageddon starting this year and continuing for twenty-four years.

1991

The world then to an end shall come
In Nineteen Hundred and Ninety-One

This is the 'final' version of Mother Shipton's little couplet, subtly updated after 1882.

1997 For excellent rabbinical reasons too complicated to mention or understand, it is said that the world must endure for 6,000 years. Oh, well, if you insist: because *Yahweh* (Jehovah) contains six letters; because the Hebrew letter 'm' occurs just six times in the book of *Genesis*; because Enoch was a member of the sixth generation descended from Adam; because the world was created in just six days; and lastly because the 6,000 years divide up so neatly into 2,000 years for the law of nature, 2,000 years for the written law and 2,000 years for the law of grace. Then, since the world was, of course, created in 4004BC (a fact attested to by numerous clerical gentlemen much more learned and religious than we are, particularly in the seventeenth century, including Archbishop Ussher), and since there was no year zero, 1997 is inarguable.

1998 This is even more undeniable than 1997. Not only is the number a magical three times the magical number of Man (or, if you prefer, the Beast) 666, but Christ was crucified (they say) in the 1,998th week of his life. Proof positive.

1999 One quatrain from Nostradamus can be translated as follows:

A great king of terror will descend from the skies,
The year 1999, seventh month,
To resuscitate the great king of Angolmois,
Around this time Mars will reign for the good cause.

A certain Stewart Robb felt this probably meant an invasion from Mars in 1999, with apocalyptic results.

2000 The double millennium; the idea being that if God had missed his cue first time, in 1000, this is a useful second chance.

2001 As for 2000—a special extra apocalypse for the pedants who remind us that a decade (or indeed a millennium) doesn't start until the year after you think.

2537 The computation of St Vincent Ferrier, who counted the verses in the Psalms and arrived at this useful number. We confess that we have not checked.

2695 The authors of this book conducted their own numerological investigation, multiplying their house-numbers together with the mystical constant pi to calculate that (if we've got the decimal places right) the world must end a few seconds before 1.43pm on 26 June 2695.

6300 Known as the Grand Climacteric. The age of 63 is called the grand climacteric of human life—mystic seven times mystic nine—and one merely multiplies this by not-so-mystic 100.

470,000 The number of people of Judah as mentioned in *I Chronicles xxi*. This has to have some vast significance, and what better than a date?

1,100,000 The number of Israelites listed in the same reference.

12,960,000 The Great Sacred Number of the Babylonians.

10,000,000,000 or thereabouts (the day and month are not specified): this, according to the *Encyclopaedia Britannica*, is when the Sun will go out.

Zymurgy

This is not so much a chapter as a last word about the brewing of our book. Under such provisional titles as *The Earth Was Created in 4004BC on the 21st of October at 9.00 in the Morning*, this distillation of ancient wisdom has been gradually assembled over a period of about a year, bringing its authors many surprises, delights and hangovers. We have kept until last what we hope is the most ludicrously misguided prediction of all, namely that 'this silly book will never sell'. (The speaker's name is suppressed to protect the innocent, though personally we feel the innocent should suffer along with the rest of us.) Far from being despondent, the authors confidently anticipate the book's rapid elevation to bestseller status—at least in that most élite of literary circles, The Relatives of David Langford and Chris Morgan—and even now we are hunting out material for a second volume. This is provisionally titled *All Right, So Maybe the Earth Wasn't Created in 4004BC on the 21st of October at 9.00 in the Morning* ... Any contributions of suitable sayings will be gratefully received by us, care of:

Webb & Bower (Publishers) Ltd.,
33 Southernhay East,
Exeter,
Devon, EX1 1NS
United Kingdom

Acknowledgements

Our thanks to Hazel Langford and Pauline Morgan, and to the following people and publications who or which have helped create this book:

Ansible, Michael Ashley, Adrian Berry, Ray Bradbury, the British Science Fiction Association, John Brookes, Charles N. Brown, John Brunner, Arthur C. Clarke, Eve Devereux, Cay Dollerup, Peter Downton, Frederick C. Dyer, Stan Eling, Alan Ferguson, Donald Franson, Martin Gardner, John Grant, Philippa Grove-Stephensen, Oliver Harris, John and Eve Harvey, W. P. Holland, Dave Holmes, John H. King, Paul Lamprill, David Lang, Denny Lien, *Locus*, Tom McDonough, Helen McNabb, D. P. M. Michael, Jackie Miller, Patrick Moore, the *New Statesman*, Maggie Noach, H. D. Poole, Andrew Porter, Roland Prosser, Ed Rattray, *SF Chronicle*, Cyril Simsa, John Sladek, Brian Stableford, *State Service*, Trevor Sturgess, Oliver Symes, *Syzygy*, *The Times Literary Supplement*, Carol Underwood, Prof. Edgar Warnhoff, Peter R. Weston, Colin Wilson, K. W. J. Wood.

Name Index

169

General Index